Make This Tonight

Make This Tonight

Recipes to Get Dinner on the Table

Tastemade

CLARKSON POTTER/
PUBLISHERS
NEW YORK

Published in the United States by Clarkson Potter/Publishers, an imprint of a Random House, a division of Penguin Random House LLC, New York.
www.clarksonpotter.com

CLARKSON POTTER is a trademark and POTTER with colophon is a registered trademark of Random House LLC.

Library of Congress Cataloging-in-Publication Data
Names: Tastemade (Firm), author.
Title: Make this tonight : recipes to get dinner on the table / Tastemade, Inc.
Identifiers: LCCN 2021021774 (print) | LCCN 2021021775 (ebook) | ISBN 9780593232187 (hardcover) | ISBN 9780593232194 (ebook)
Subjects: LCSH: Cooking. | Quick and easy cooking. | LCGFT: Cookbooks.
Classification: LCC TX714 .T376 2022 (print) | LCC TX714 (ebook) | DDC 641.5–dc23
LC record available at https://lccn.loc.gov/2021021774
LC ebook record available at https://lccn.loc.gov/2021021775

ISBN 978-0-593-23218-7
Ebook ISBN 978-0-593-23219-4

Printed in China

Creative direction: Amanda Dameron, Sarah Anne Bargatze, and Paul Delmont
Project oversight: Tyler Wildermuth and Jeremy Strauss
Photographer: Paul Delmont and Ashley Corbin-Teich

Editor: Lydia O'Brien
Contributing editor: Amanda Englander
Designer: Bryce de Flamand
Production editor: Joyce Wong
Production manager: Jessica Heim
Composition: Merri Ann Morrell, Hannah Hunt, and Zoe Tokushige
Copyeditor: Kate Slate
Indexer: Elizabeth Parson
Marketer: Chloe Aryeh
Publicist: Natalie Yera

10 9 8 7 6 5 4 3 2 1

First Edition

*This book is dedicated to
our passionate Tastemade
community, whose appetite for
good food and great company
inspires us every day.*

Contents

Introduction

Tastemade is a community of creative and passionate people. We are a global company with studios all over the world. We are storytellers, striving to capture moments of hope, adventure, and art. We work together to surface voices and creations that represent the rich tapestry of cultures. We know that "good taste" means nothing without respect—respect for quality ingredients, for cultures around the world, and for sound techniques performed by capable hands. We believe the world is delicious and sharing a meal with others is the best way to become a truly global citizen. At Tastemade, we believe there is more in this world that unites us than divides us, and that good food is one of those common threads.

As part of that common thread, there's one question we all have to answer every single day: What's for dinner? Sometimes you're excited at the prospect of preparing a feast, perhaps inviting company over to share in the fun of cooking and certainly of eating. Other times you need a quick, easy solution because you're too busy or distracted to stop to think about it. Sometimes you want familiar flavors and the comforts of a dish you grew up with. Other times you want to try something new you've only ever heard about. However you feel, whatever you crave, however much time you have on any given day, and whatever other circumstances there are, you know it will end with dinner. Let's answer that question together, shall we?

About This Book

In your hands, you hold our very first cookbook. We gathered 100 recipes from our network of professional chefs and self-taught cooks. With lots of new and exciting any-day-of-the-week inspiration, we've ventured to help you answer the question of what to make. We appreciate the joy of a great plate of food, and we know a lot of paths to achieve that end result. We encourage you to explore the culinary offerings of our community and make them your own. Cooking is a lifelong journey, and this book is a tool for anyone curious and eager to get comfortable in the kitchen. We hope you'll enjoy learning from those who contributed recipes and shared their personal connections to many regions of the world as we traverse the globe through this compendium of good food, good stories, and good people.

The recipes in *Make This Tonight* reflect a mix of family tradition, far-flung inspiration, appreciation of heritage, and most of all a healthy dose of fun and exploration. This book is a starter kit for new ways of enjoying food, meant to empower you to create explosively flavorful dishes that will enrich your kitchen and cultivate your culinary soul. It's a primer for learning to love to cook. We hope to convince you of our own philosophy: that life's true victories—both in and out of the kitchen—come when your sources are global, richly varied, and authentic, and that these victories are 100 percent achievable every day. Our goal is to show you that preparing delicious food and gathering at the table don't need to be difficult endeavors. With a bit of practice, they will become second nature to you, and you'll be able to feed yourself and your family and friends every night.

We have organized this book into sections by main ingredient—vegetables, eggs, grains, meat, and more. Each chapter will not only provide new ways for you to enjoy ingredients that you might have grown up with but will also contain countless opportunities for culinary exploration. Some of the recipes will feature familiar flavors, while others will encourage you to expand your spice cabinet or travel to faraway lands via your taste buds. At Tastemade, we are driven by constant curiosity. With *Make This Tonight*, you'll learn some of the ways we feed that curiosity—stocking a new-to-us spice, letting something ferment in our cupboard. These recipes are compelling yet comforting, exciting yet approachable. They can make any night an adventure or cozy and familiar.

Equipment and Ingredients

When it comes to cooking, you can make or break not only the flavor of the dish but also how much *fun* you have with creating it based on the tools and ingredients at your disposal. Mixing a salad in a bowl that's too small will totally cramp your style when you're trying to get the dressing properly distributed. The wrong kind of salt can ruin a really good thing. Here is a list of some kitchen essentials you need to create great food—nothing too fancy or frivolous, just the basics for getting started.

POTS AND PANS: We recommend at least one of each of the following: a medium saucepan, a large soup pot, an 8- to 10-inch skillet, a 10- to 12-inch cast-iron skillet, and a good Dutch oven. The most important thing to remember here is to focus on quality over quantity. Durable and well-made pots and pans will help your food cook more evenly and consistently, plus they'll last a lifetime.

SHEET PANS: We recommend keeping a few half-sheet and quarter-sheet pans handy. Besides the fact that plenty of recipes in this book allow you to cook the meal entirely on a sheet pan, sheet pans are also great tools for freezing extra cookies, assembling your mise en place bowls, reheating leftovers, and organizing kitchen tools. You will not believe how easy the cleanup from an entire meal will be whenever you go this route.

BAKING DISHES AND PANS: A good starting bakeware collection includes a 9 × 13-inch baking dish, an 8 × 8-inch baking dish, a pie plate, and a 9-inch cake pan.

KNIVES: You do not need many knives to get started in the kitchen, but you do need a few good ones. On a tight budget, a good chef's knife is the one worth investing in. Start with a 6- or 7-inch chef's knife with a decent amount of weight and add a 3- to 4-inch paring knife next. These two knives alone will get you through this book and any recipe.

CANNING JARS: With a chapter full of recipes for fermentation and home-made preserves, of course we're going to advise stocking canning jars of all shapes and sizes. Not only can you use them for canning, but we also love to use them as a sustainable way to store leftovers, condiments, sauces, spices, and other dry goods.

MICROPLANE GRATER: Use it to grate garlic or ginger for dressings or marinades, to zest fresh citrus, or to grate hard cheeses like Parmesan.

BOX GRATER: This is a great tool for grating large vegetables, chocolate, and especially cheeses, which are often much more affordable and better-quality when purchased as a block and shredded or grated at home.

VEGETABLE PEELER: This tool will save you precious prep time, and it's not just for vegetables—use it for peeling strips of citrus zest, for creating delicate shavings of chocolate, or for creating slivers of cheese for a salad. We recommend a Y-style vegetable peeler.

SILICONE SPATULAS: A few sturdy heatproof silicone spatulas will help you mix, flip, toss, and scrape down the sides of bowls with ease.

WOODEN SPOONS: A wooden spoon is the best tool for stirring sauces, soups, and stews, plus it's perfect for scraping up all the tasty bits from the bottom of a pan. One or two that you care for well is all you need.

ROLLING PIN: We recommend a French-style pin—a simple cylinder of wood with tapered ends on each side. It lends the most control and if you oil it regularly, it will last for years.

COLANDER: A large sturdy one with smallish holes is the best buy, since you can use it for everything from washing berries and grains to draining pasta.

FINE MESH SIEVE: We like a medium-size one with a handle for rinsing smaller grains and dusting confectioners' sugar on our desserts.

FOOD PROCESSOR: We use our food processor all the time. If you cook often, it will practically be your sous-chef, blending smooth dips like hummus and sauces like pesto. It can also chop veggies as finely as you might need them for salsas or for the base of soup or stew.

FLOUR: Using the correct type for a given recipe will really influence the outcome. All-purpose flour almost always does the trick, but cake or pastry flour is also worth experimenting with if you want to flex in the baking space. Bread will require bread flour, which is higher in gluten. We also love rye flour for its earthy flavor and dense texture.

OIL: For the most part, when cooking with olive oil, any type will work, though we favor extra-virgin for its flavor and mouthfeel. When using olive oil in a salad dressing or as garnish (i.e., raw), definitely stick with evoo. We also use neutral oil often for its high smoke point. Avocado, vegetable, canola, grapeseed, safflower . . . whatever you have handy.

VINEGAR: Vinegars are incredibly versatile and affordable, and they have great shelf life. We recommend keeping white wine vinegar, distilled white vinegar, apple cider vinegar, balsamic vinegar, and red wine vinegar. Having a few of these should cover all of your canning, pickling, and salad dressing needs. And in most cases, you can easily substitute whatever vinegar you have on hand for another.

SALT: We like Diamond Crystal kosher salt to season or cook with, and Maldon flaky sea salt for finishing. The size of the kosher salt grains are perfect for cooking, while the crunch of Maldon will take finishing to the next level.

SPICES: We consider the spice cabinet our window to the world—a way to travel without leaving home. Spices are also a way to infuse satisfying flavor into your cooking without a miles-long shopping list. They can be expensive, so buy them as you need them and rest assured that a little goes a long way. When possible, we recommend sourcing them from smaller, sustainability-minded purveyors, such as Diaspora Co. or Burlap & Barrel. We love all our spices, but this is a short list of favorites to get you started.

Black peppercorns	Nutmeg
Cinnamon, ground	Paprika
Cumin, ground	Red pepper flakes, crushed
Curry powder	Thyme
Ginger, ground	Turmeric, ground

SAUCES, CONDIMENTS, AND SPREADS: Similar to spices, these flavor bombs can take you from "Dinner. Now." to "Dinner? Wow!" Again, try buying these one at a time as you need them. The more you cook, the happier you'll be to have them in your pantry; they're all versatile and useful in their own ways.

Fish sauce (we like Red Boat)	Soy sauce
Hot sauce	Tahini
Miso	

Vegetables

Roasted Garlic Baba Ghanoush

If you can make a homemade dip that's suitable for dredging with a sturdy chip, a crisp vegetable, or a nice chunk of bread, you're set up for a great round of hosting, potlucking, and/or picnicking success. If you can make a dip as addictive as this one—and one of the best ways to eat eggplant— you've won the game entirely. Smoky, garlicky, and super savory, you're in for a treat. We like to mix ours up by hand for a rustic texture, but feel free to make your baba ghanoush in a food processor for a smoother finish.

SERVES 3 OR 4

1 head garlic

2 large eggplants (about 1½ pound)

¼ cup tahini

2 tablespoons extra-virgin olive oil

1½ teaspoons kosher salt

Juice of ½ lemon

Olives, for serving (optional)

Sumac, for serving (optional)

Parsley, for serving (optional)

Preheat the oven to 400°F. Line a sheet pan with parchment paper or foil.

Cut off the top of the head of garlic crosswise to reveal the cloves. Wrap in foil, place on the sheet pan, and roast until very fragrant, 30 to 40 minutes. Remove, carefully unwrap, and let cool slightly.

Meanwhile, turn a gas burner to medium heat. Using heatproof tongs, place one eggplant directly on the grate. Cook, rotating the eggplant about 90 degrees every 2 minutes, until blackened with the skin beginning to fall off, 10 to 12 minutes total. Repeat with the second eggplant. Let the eggplants cool slightly. (Alternatively, if you don't have a gas stove, you can use the same process on a grill, or in the oven with a rack next to the broiler.)

When the eggplants are cool enough to handle, remove most of the charred skin, being careful not to sacrifice any of the flesh. Roughly chop the flesh to loosen it and scoop it out into a medium bowl.

Squeeze the roasted garlic cloves out of their skins into the bowl, stirring to break them up and incorporate into the eggplant. Stir in the tahini, olive oil, salt, and lemon juice.

If desired, garnish the baba ghanoush with olives, sumac, and parsley before serving. Store refrigerated in an airtight container for up to 5 days.

Vegetables

Loaded Sweet Potato Nachos with Crema

Sometimes you just need a decadent food mountain that satisfies and stupefies. There is no judgment here, and you need look no further. Sliced sweet potatoes stand in for tortilla chips and we pile them high with all our favorite nacho fixin's: black beans, corn, red peppers, jalapeño, scallions, and last, but never, ever least, cheese. Avocado crema finishes it all off—feel free to make it your own with whatever spices you're in the mood for. Garlic, oregano, paprika, cumin, and any of your other favorites are all welcome.

SERVES 4 TO 6

2 sweet potatoes, scrubbed, peeled, and cut into ½-inch-thick slices

1 tablespoon extra-virgin olive oil

½ teaspoon kosher salt, plus more to taste

2 avocados, halved

1 cup sour cream

Juice of 1 lime

Freshly ground black pepper

1½ cups shredded cheddar or pepper Jack cheese

¼ cup canned black beans, drained and rinsed

¼ cup frozen roasted corn, thawed

¼ cup chopped roasted red pepper

2 scallions, thinly sliced

1 jalapeño, thinly sliced

3 tablespoons crumbled Cotija cheese

¼ cup fresh cilantro

Preheat the oven to 400°F.

Divide the sweet potatoes between two sheet pans, arranging the slices in a single layer. Drizzle with the olive oil, sprinkle with the salt, and toss to coat. Bake until golden brown and crispy, 20 to 25 minutes, flipping halfway through.

Meanwhile, scoop the avocados into a food processor. Add the sour cream and lime juice and pulse until smooth. If the crema is too thick, add water, 1 tablespoon at a time, until the desired consistency is reached. Taste and add salt and black pepper as desired. Transfer the crema to a small bowl and refrigerate until ready to serve.

Place the roasted sweet potatoes onto a parchment-lined sheet pan. Scatter on the cheddar, black beans, corn, roasted pepper, scallions, and jalapeño. Bake until the cheese is melted, 6 to 8 minutes.

Top the nachos with the avocado crema, Cotija, and cilantro. Serve.

Whole Roasted Za'atar Cauliflower with Tahini Sauce

If you really want to make an impression, plopping a whole head of perfectly seasoned roasted cauliflower onto the dinner table is one way. And this bold recipe will change the mind of anyone who's skeptical of this vegetable. With the right spices—including a generous dose of salty, smoky, nutty, tangy za'atar, a Mediterranean spice blend—and a good crisping in the oven, this otherwise bland vegetable takes on a new life. The tahini sauce on top makes it even more deserving of the spotlight. Just cut into it gently to scoop and serve.

SERVES 3 OR 4

For the cauliflower

1 head cauliflower

½ cup za'atar

2 teaspoons kosher salt

1 teaspoon garlic powder

1 teaspoon onion powder

1 teaspoon sumac

1 teaspoon paprika

1 teaspoon freshly ground black pepper

2 tablespoons extra-virgin olive oil

For the tahini sauce

½ cup tahini

Juice of 1 lemon

2 tablespoons extra-virgin olive oil

1 teaspoon kosher salt

2 garlic cloves, peeled

MAKE THE CAULIFLOWER: Preheat the oven to 400°F. Line a sheet pan with parchment paper.

Use a large knife to trim the outer green leaves from the cauliflower and trim the stalk by cutting inward toward the core in a circular motion, being careful not to cut into the head—just cut the stalk enough so the head sits flat.

Bring a large pot of salted water to a boil. Carefully add the cauliflower and cook until knife tender, about 5 minutes. Use tongs to remove the cauliflower, gently shaking off the water, and transfer the cauliflower to the prepared sheet pan. Pat dry.

In a small bowl, stir together the za'atar, salt, garlic powder, onion powder, sumac, paprika, and pepper. Drizzle the olive oil over the cauliflower. Sprinkle on the spice mixture and rub to coat well, being sure it gets into the nooks and crannies and covers the underside, too.

Roast the cauliflower until golden brown, about 12 minutes.

MEANWHILE, MAKE THE TAHINI SAUCE: In a food processor or blender, combine the tahini, lemon juice, olive oil, salt, and garlic. Pulse until smooth.

Serve the cauliflower family-style with the tahini sauce alongside.

Mushroom Salad

Mushrooms don't often get to be the star of the show in side-dish world, but when they are combined with walnuts and bread crumbs for crunch and an assertive dressing in this warm salad, they might just be our new favorite thing. Tons of nutrients, super healthy, eye-popping color from other fresh veggies, and leftovers that only get more delicious in the refrigerator . . . what's not to love? For something more filling, try serving the mushroom mix on top of greens or toast.

SERVES 4 TO 6

2 tablespoons extra-virgin olive oil, plus more as needed

¼ cup chopped walnuts

¼ cup panko bread crumbs

2 portobello mushroom caps, sliced

1 pound mixed mushrooms, such as shiitake, oyster, and/or white, sliced

Kosher salt

2 carrots, shaved into ribbons (see Note)

White wine vinegar

10 ounces cherry tomatoes, halved

2 tablespoons fresh parsley

2 tablespoons fresh basil

For the dressing

¼ cup balsamic vinegar

¼ cup extra-virgin olive oil

Kosher salt and freshly ground black pepper

In a medium skillet, heat the olive oil over medium-low heat. Add the walnuts and panko and cook, stirring, until the bread crumbs are golden brown, about 5 minutes. Transfer the mixture to a small bowl and set aside.

Add the portobello mushrooms and the mixed mushrooms to the skillet and increase the heat to medium-high. Season with salt. Cook, stirring, until the mushrooms begin to take on color and caramelize, 7 to 9 minutes. Transfer to a serving bowl.

If the skillet seems dry, add another splash of olive oil. Add the carrot ribbons over medium-high heat and season with salt. Cook, stirring, until softened, about 2 minutes. Gently stir in a splash of vinegar and then remove from the heat.

Add the carrots to the bowl with the mushrooms. Add the tomatoes, parsley, and basil and toss to combine.

MAKE THE DRESSING: In a small bowl, whisk together the balsamic vinegar and olive oil. Season to taste with salt and pepper. Pour the dressing over the salad and toss to coat. Refrigerate the salad for at least 30 minutes or up to 6 hours.

Scatter the walnut-panko mixture over the salad just before serving.

NOTE: Use a vegetable peeler to shave the carrots into ribbons—just make sure you scrub the carrots first or peel off the top layer.

Beet Hummus

Sure, you've had hummus before, but have you had beet *hummus? The sweetness of the beets comes out after a roast in the oven, adding a pleasant layer of flavor to this otherwise creamy, savory dip. Plus, that vibrant magenta hue looks stunning on any table. If you can get your hands on pomegranate molasses, it will add a worthwhile extra zippiness, too. Scoop up this hummus with assorted veggies, crackers, or whatever bread you like best.*

SERVES 4 TO 6

4 medium red beets, scrubbed (about 1 to 1½ pounds)

2 tablespoons extra-virgin olive oil

2 teaspoons kosher salt, plus more to taste

1 (15.5-ounce) can chickpeas, drained and rinsed

¼ cup tahini

2 tablespoons fresh lemon juice

2 tablespoons pomegranate molasses (optional)

1 teaspoon ground cumin

½ teaspoon freshly ground black pepper, plus more to taste

Sesame seeds, for serving

Dill, for serving

Preheat the oven to 400°F.

On a sheet pan, toss the beets with the olive oil and 1 teaspoon of the salt. Roast until knife tender, 45 minutes to 1 hour. Remove from the oven and, working quickly, use a kitchen towel or paper towels to gently rub the skins off the beets. Let them cool slightly, then roughly chop. Let cool completely.

Transfer the chopped beets to a food processor and pulse until mostly smooth. Add the chickpeas, tahini, lemon juice, pomegranate molasses (if using), cumin, the remaining 1 teaspoon salt, and the pepper. Pulse until the mixture is completely smooth. (If the hummus is too thick, drizzle in water 1 tablespoon at a time, with the motor running to smooth it out.) Taste and season with additional salt and pepper as desired. Serve with sesame seeds and dill.

Transfer the hummus to a serving bowl. Store refrigerated in an airtight container for up to 1 week.

Any-Greens Caesar Salad

If there is a person in your life who claims to hate salad, we recommend trying out this recipe on them. The lettuce is the perfect canvas for this (if we do say so ourselves) Caesar dressing, which can be stored for up to a week in the fridge. We swap out the raw egg for a hard-boiled yolk, but whatever you do, don't shy away from the anchovies—not only are they the essence of any Caesar, but they also deliver savory-umami depth of flavor. While a Caesar usually calls for romaine lettuce, feel free to use any other sturdy green you have around. Kale and Little Gem are always crowd-pleasers!

SERVES 2 TO 4

6 oil-packed anchovy fillets, drained, plus more, chopped, for serving (optional)

4 garlic cloves, finely minced or pressed

1 hard-boiled egg yolk

2 tablespoons red wine vinegar

Juice of 1 lemon

1 tablespoon grainy Dijon mustard

1 cup freshly grated Parmesan cheese

½ teaspoon kosher salt, plus more to taste

⅛ teaspoon freshly ground black pepper, plus more to taste

½ cup extra-virgin olive oil

3 cups chopped romaine lettuce

Garlic toasts, for serving

In a food processor, combine the anchovies, garlic, and egg yolk and process until a smooth paste forms. Add the vinegar, lemon juice, mustard, the ½ cup of the Parmesan, salt, and pepper and pulse to combine. With the machine running, gradually drizzle in the olive oil until smooth. Taste and adjust the salt and pepper as desired.

Place the lettuce in a large serving bowl, pour the dressing over the top, and toss to coat. Sprinkle with the ½ cup of Parmesan and crumbled garlic toasts. If desired, garnish with chopped anchovies. Serve.

Japanese Potato Salad

Japanese versions of Western foods are called yōshoku, *and potato salad is a popular item in that category. It always has lots of crunchy veggies that contrast with the creamy-chunky texture of the lightly mashed potatoes. Our version is fresh, crisp, and addictive—green apple, cucumber, carrot, and scallion work together delightfully, unexpectedly. Spread it on toast or use it in a sandwich for tartness and oomph. If you have a mandoline, now is a great time to pull it out to get consistent, paper-thin slices.*

SERVES 4

1 English cucumber, thinly sliced

Kosher salt

2 pounds Yukon Gold potatoes, peeled and cut into 1½-inch cubes

1 large carrot, julienned

½ medium yellow onion, thinly sliced

1 crisp tart apple (such as Pink Lady or Granny Smith), diced

1½ cups mayonnaise

1 teaspoon hot, spicy brown, or sweet German mustard

Freshly ground black pepper

Thinly sliced scallion, for serving

Line a plate with a kitchen towel. Arrange the cucumber in a single layer on top. Sprinkle the cucumber liberally with salt, place another towel on top, and let sit for 1 hour.

Meanwhile, bring a large pot of water to a boil. Add the potatoes and cook until fork-tender, about 20 minutes. Drain, lightly mash, and let cool.

Fill a medium bowl with water to rinse the excess salt off the salted cucumbers before transferring them to a towel. Gather up the ends of the towel beneath the cucumbers and gently squeeze the water out of them, being careful not to break them. Transfer to a large bowl.

Add the potatoes, carrot, onion, apple, mayonnaise, mustard, and salt and pepper to taste. Toss to coat. Refrigerate the potato salad for at least 1 hour before serving.

Top with thinly sliced scallion.

Ratatouille on Grilled Bread

Ratatouille takes your bounty of garden vegetables—eggplant, bell peppers, squash—and combines it with blissfully jammy tomatoes and a bundle of basil (just add kitchen string) to create a perfect party of summer flavors. While often eaten like a stew, we've decided to give our ratatouille its own personalized vehicle by spooning it on top of toast. You want something sturdy to hold up to this saucy stuff—just about any crusty loaf will do, but we especially love ciabatta or sourdough, like the one on page 243.

SERVES 6 TO 8

8 ounces eggplant, cut into ½-inch pieces

1½ teaspoons kosher salt, plus more to taste

4½ tablespoons extra-virgin olive oil, plus more for serving

1 leek, sliced

6 garlic cloves, minced

1 teaspoon crushed red pepper flakes

2 ounces fresh basil sprigs, tied with kitchen string, plus leaves for serving

8 ounces bell pepper, cut into ½-inch pieces

8 ounces summer squash, cut into ½-inch pieces

10 ounces cherry tomatoes, halved

Freshly ground black pepper

1 loaf crusty bread, sliced

In a large bowl, toss the eggplant with 1½ teaspoons salt. Let sit for about 30 minutes, then use a paper towel to wipe off the salt and pat dry.

In a large saucepan, heat 1½ tablespoons of the olive oil over medium heat. Add the eggplant and cook, stirring occasionally, until golden and tender, about 15 minutes. Use a slotted spoon to transfer the eggplant to a plate.

Heat another 2 tablespoons of the olive oil in the same pan. Add the leek and cook, stirring occasionally, until soft and translucent, 8 to 10 minutes.

Add half of the garlic, the pepper flakes, and the bundle of basil. Cook, stirring, until fragrant, about 1 minute. Add the bell pepper and cook, stirring occasionally, until softened, 3 to 5 minutes.

Add the squash and tomatoes and continue to cook, stirring occasionally, until the flavors meld and the bell pepper and squash are soft (but not falling apart), about 10 minutes more.

Return the eggplant to the pot and cook for another minute to warm through.

Carefully remove the bundle of basil, squeeze out any liquid back into the ratatouille, and discard the basil bundle. Stir in the remaining garlic. Taste and add salt and black pepper as desired.

Meanwhile, in a grill pan or large skillet, heat the remaining 1 tablespoon olive oil over medium heat. Working in batches, add the bread slices in a single layer and cook until golden and crisp, about 30 seconds per side. Repeat with the remaining bread slices, adding more olive oil to the skillet as needed.

To serve, spoon the ratatouille over the toasts. Drizzle with some olive oil and sprinkle on basil leaves.

Cheesy Bubble and Squeak

This simple British dish is perfect for putting leftover vegetables like potatoes and cabbage to work. We've updated the traditional recipe by adding mustard powder and miso umami bombs, and an outer layer of bread crumbs for crunch. But if you don't have leftovers and want to make this from scratch, a quick steam will get your veggies ready for their new lives as crisp, cheesy patties. Change it up with sweet potatoes, sticky Japanese sweet potatoes (and skip the egg if you go for the latter), or cauliflower in place of the cabbage. And if you'd like to go beyond the bounds of cheddar, any good melting cheese like Muenster or pepper Jack would work. Make a meal of it by adding eggs and a nice big salad, too.

MAKES 6 PATTIES

2 teaspoons miso or
1 teaspoon kosher salt

1 teaspoon hot water

1 large egg

⅛ teaspoon mustard powder (optional)

2 to 3 large russet potatoes, steamed, sliced, and lightly mashed (about 3 cups)

Kosher salt and freshly ground black pepper

½ cup shredded white cheddar cheese

¼ head green or napa cabbage, steamed and cut into ¼-inch-wide strips (about 1¾ cups)

½ cup bread crumbs

1 tablespoon vegetable oil or extra-virgin olive oil, plus more as needed

In a large bowl, stir together the miso and hot water. Add the egg and mustard powder, if using. Add the potatoes and stir to combine, mashing them lightly. Season with salt and pepper. Fold in the cheddar and cabbage. Divide the mixture evenly into 6 patties, each about ½ inch thick.

Spread the bread crumbs on a small plate. Working with one patty at a time, lightly dip each into the bread crumbs to coat both sides, pressing to adhere.

CONTINUED

In a large skillet, heat the oil over medium-high heat. Working in batches, add the patties, leaving ½ inch between them. Reduce the heat to medium-low and cook until the undersides are crispy and slightly browned, 2 to 3 minutes. Flip and continue to cook until both sides are crispy and slightly browned, 2 to 3 minutes more. Transfer the finished patties to a serving plate and repeat with the remainder, adding more oil to the skillet between batches as needed.

Arrange on a platter and serve.

How to Steam Vegetables

Fill a medium saucepan with ½ inch of water and bring to a boil. Place the whole potatoes in a steamer basket (cut the potatoes to fit as needed). Add the cabbage, cut into wedges, in a single layer on top. Cover and reduce the heat to simmer. After 5 minutes, the cabbage should be softened; remove it and let the potatoes continue to steam for another 8 to 12 minutes until fork-tender.

Let the vegetables cool enough so you can handle them. Slice the potatoes into rounds and mash them lightly. Discard the cabbage's core and slice the leaves into ¼-inch-wide strips.

If you don't have a steamer basket, you can improvise with a small trivet with a shallow dish set on top to hold the vegetables.

Kimchi Pancakes

Anju *is the Korean tradition of serving alcohol with* banchan, *the series of small side dishes that accompany a meal.* Kimchi-buchimgae *are commonly found in this scenario—they're a very popular type of* buchimgae, *the Korean word for pancake. We think kimchi makes just about everything better. And if* you *love kimchi, you will love these pancakes, which are absolutely brimming with flavor. They even get an extra hit of protein from the tofu we crumbled in. The delicious, caramelized crust encases a soft, fluffy—and dare we say briny—interior.*

MAKES FOUR 6-INCH PANCAKES

For the pancakes

1 cup all-purpose flour

¼ cup cornstarch

1 teaspoon baking powder

1 teaspoon onion powder

½ teaspoon garlic powder

¼ teaspoon kosher salt

½ teaspoon sugar

1 cup ice water

1 cup coarsely chopped Super Garlic Kimchi (page 251) or store-bought

1 to 2 tablespoons brine from the kimchi

2 ounces firm tofu, drained and crumbled (about ¼ cup) (see Note)

2 scallions, thinly sliced

1 tablespoon vegetable oil, plus more as needed

For the dipping sauce

1 tablespoon soy sauce

1 tablespoon rice vinegar

Sesame seeds

2 scallions, thinly sliced

MAKE THE PANCAKES: In a large bowl, mix together the flour, cornstarch, baking powder, onion powder, garlic powder, salt, and sugar. Pour in the ice water. Stir in the kimchi and brine. Add the crumbled tofu and half of the scallions.

In a large skillet, heat the oil over medium-high heat. Working in batches, pour in about ⅓ cup of the batter to make each pancake. Cook until the bottom is golden brown and bubbles begin to appear on the surface, 2 to 3 minutes. Flip and continue to cook until golden brown on both sides, 2 to 3 minutes more. Transfer to a serving platter. Repeat with the remaining batter, adding more oil to the skillet between batches as needed.

Vegetables

CONTINUED

MEANWHILE, MAKE THE DIPPING SAUCE: In a small bowl, whisk together the soy sauce, rice vinegar, a pinch of sesame seeds, and scallions.

Garnish the kimchi pancakes with the remaining scallions. Serve with the dipping sauce alongside.

NOTE: To drain tofu, after removing it from the container, place it on a plate sandwiched between double-layers of paper towels. Place something heavy on top, like a skillet, and let it sit for about 15 minutes.

Cheesy, Creamy Chickpeas

Canned chickpeas might not seem like dinner, but when you combine them with pops of super-flavor and add cheese, well, you have a no-brainer any night of the week. You can treat these comforting chickpeas as a side dish or the main event, especially with a salad to accompany them and some warm bread for dipping.

SERVES 4 TO 6

2 tablespoons unsalted butter or extra-virgin olive oil

1 medium yellow onion, diced

Kosher salt and freshly ground black pepper

2 garlic cloves, minced

¼ to ½ teaspoon cayenne pepper

2 teaspoons prepared horseradish

2 teaspoons Dijon mustard

2 tablespoons all-purpose flour

2 (15.5-ounce) cans chickpeas, drained and rinsed

1 cup vegetable broth

¼ cup cream cheese

1½ cups shredded Monterey Jack, cheddar, or a cheese blend

½ cup shredded Parmesan cheese

Chopped fresh parsley, for serving (optional)

Crushed red pepper flakes, for serving (optional)

Preheat the oven to 400°F.

In a large ovenproof skillet, melt the butter over medium heat. Add the onion and cook, stirring occasionally, until soft and translucent, 7 to 10 minutes. Season with salt and black pepper. Add the garlic and cook until fragrant, about 1 minute more. Add the cayenne, horseradish, mustard, and flour and cook, stirring, until the flour is lightly toasted and golden, 2 to 3 minutes.

Stir in the chickpeas and vegetable broth. Continue cooking until the chickpeas are beginning to fall apart, 10 to 12 minutes. Add more broth or water if it gets too pasty. Use the back of a wooden spoon or a potato masher to mash one-quarter to one-third of the chickpeas.

Add the cream cheese and stir to melt and combine, 1 to 2 minutes. Stir in the Monterey Jack to melt and combine, another 1 to 2 minutes. Season with salt and black pepper. Sprinkle the Parmesan over the top.

Transfer to the oven and bake until the liquid is bubbling and the top is golden brown, about 15 minutes. If desired, garnish with parsley and/or pepper flakes.

Vegetables

Spaghetti Squash Cacio e Pepe

Spaghetti squash is a vegetable star—when roasted, its flesh pulls into (you guessed it) spaghetti-like strands that are a perfect canvas on which to build bold flavors. Yes, we've tossed it with the beloved Italian pasta condiment here, but with cashew butter, oat milk, and nutritional yeast coming together to make a vegan cacio, this dish is a gift to gluten-free eaters, dairy-free eaters, and omnivores alike—and it's as deliciously decadent as can be. Any blender, from full-size to mini bullet, is the best way to pull this sauce together in a flash.

SERVES 2 TO 4

Extra-virgin olive oil

1 large spaghetti squash (2 to 3 pounds), halved lengthwise and seeded

¼ cup cashew butter

¼ cup nutritional yeast

1 tablespoon potato starch

¼ cup plain oat milk

2 tablespoons white miso

1 garlic clove, peeled

Sea salt

1 tablespoon freshly ground black pepper, plus more for serving

Preheat the oven to 375°F. Line a sheet pan with parchment paper and drizzle the parchment with olive oil.

Place the squash cut-side down on the sheet pan. Roast until the squash is fork-tender and the flesh is golden, 30 to 40 minutes. Remove from the oven and let cool.

Meanwhile, in a blender, combine the cashew butter, nutritional yeast, potato starch, oat milk, miso, garlic, a pinch of salt, and the pepper. Blend on high until smooth, 1 to 2 minutes.

Pour the sauce into a small saucepan. Set over low heat and cook, stirring occasionally, for 12 to 15 minutes to thicken.

Use a fork to shred the squash flesh into strands. Transfer the strands to a large bowl. Pour in the sauce and toss to coat. Top with additional pepper to taste and serve.

Eggs

Spicy Turmeric Shakshuka

Shakshuka is one of those dishes that just never gets old, especially since it's endlessly adaptable. Easy to put together, it's perfect for brunch because you can pop it in the oven to finish while you stir up mimosas and slice some crusty bread for dipping (a must). Then straight to the table it goes, served from the skillet it was cooked in. Our shakshuka features a healthy dose of turmeric for a gorgeous golden-orange color and delicious spiced floral flavor that pairs beautifully with the sweet potatoes, along with the traditional tomato and bell pepper base. If you want to experiment with a richer flavor for cozy winter mornings, you can add ras el hanout, a spice blend common in North African cooking—use half the amount of turmeric to balance everything out.

SERVES 4 TO 6

2 tablespoons extra-virgin olive oil, plus more as needed

1 medium yellow onion, diced

1 medium sweet potato, peeled and diced

1 red bell pepper, diced

4 garlic cloves, minced

1½ teaspoons ground turmeric

1 teaspoon paprika

½ teaspoon ground cumin

½ teaspoon kosher salt

¼ teaspoon freshly ground black pepper

1 (28-ounce) can diced tomatoes

½ to 1 teaspoon hot sauce, plus more for serving

6 large eggs

⅓ cup crumbled feta cheese

Fresh cilantro or parsley leaves, for serving

Toasted cumin seeds, for serving (optional)

Sliced crusty bread, for serving

Preheat the oven to 400°F.

In a large ovenproof skillet, heat the olive oil over medium heat. Add the onion, sweet potato, and bell pepper and cook, stirring occasionally, until the onion is beginning to caramelize and the sweet potato is soft, 15 to 20 minutes.

Add the garlic and continue to cook until fragrant, about 2 minutes more. Toss in the turmeric, paprika, ground cumin, salt, and black pepper. Cook, stirring constantly, until the spices are fragrant, about 1 minute. Mix in the tomatoes and their juices. (If you like a looser shakshuka, you can add a splash of water here.) Stir in the hot sauce and bring the mixture to a simmer over medium heat. Cook until the mixture is warmed through and thickened, 10 to 12 minutes.

Using the back of a spoon or a measuring cup, create 6 wells on the surface of the shakshuka. Carefully crack one egg into each well.

Transfer to the oven and bake the shakshuka until the egg whites have set and the yolks are still slightly jammy, about 10 minutes. (If you prefer more well-done yolks, bake a few minutes longer.)

Remove the shakshuka from the oven and immediately sprinkle on the feta, herbs, and toasted cumin seeds (if using). Serve with additional hot sauce and crusty bread alongside.

Egg, Havarti, and Greens Pizza

Eggs on pizza are rich, decadent, and, in our opinion, underused. When you add Havarti cheese to the mix, it's game over. Rather than tell you what meal this pizza is most appropriate for, we'll promise you it's the right decision no matter the time of day. If these toppings aren't for you, swap them out for whatever you like. Eggs would be just as delicious on top of a cheese and pepperoni pizza drizzled with some hot chili oil right out of the oven, or underneath a huge pile of arugula dressed with a touch of olive oil and lemon juice. No matter what, this homemade crust is a winner and you can top it with whatever you please in the future.

SERVES 4 TO 6

For the dough

1⅓ cups lukewarm water

1½ teaspoons instant yeast

2¼ teaspoons kosher salt

1½ teaspoons sugar

2 tablespoons extra-virgin olive oil, plus more for the bowl

3¼ cups all-purpose flour

For the pizzas

1 tablespoon extra-virgin olive oil, plus more for drizzling

1 small yellow onion, diced

2 garlic cloves, thinly sliced

2 bunches kale or spinach, roughly chopped (about 6 cups)

Juice of 1 lemon

¼ teaspoon crushed red pepper flakes, plus more to taste

6 to 8 slices Havarti cheese, torn

¼ cup freshly shaved Parmesan cheese, plus more for serving

6 large eggs

Kosher salt and freshly ground black pepper

MAKE THE DOUGH: In a large bowl, stir together the water, yeast, salt, sugar, and olive oil. Add the flour and stir until the mixture is smooth and no dry streaks remain. Place in an oiled bowl, cover with a clean kitchen towel, and set aside at room temperature to rise until doubled in size, about 2 hours.

About 1 hour into the dough rising, position a rack in the lower third of the oven and preheat the oven to 450°F. Place a pizza stone or upside-down sheet pan on the oven rack to preheat as well.

CONTINUED

MEANWHILE, MAKE THE PIZZAS: About 30 minutes before the dough is finished rising, in a large skillet, heat the olive oil over medium heat. Add the onion and cook, stirring occasionally, until beginning to soften, about 5 minutes. Toss in the garlic and cook until golden and fragrant, about 2 minutes. Mix in the greens and cook, stirring, until wilted, 4 to 6 minutes. Remove the skillet from the heat. Stir in the lemon juice and pepper flakes.

When the dough has risen, divide it into 2 or 3 balls depending on your desired pizza size—dividing it into 2 balls will give you two 12-inch pizzas, and dividing it into 3 balls will give you three 8-inch pizzas.

Working with one dough ball at a time, oil your hands and gently roll out and stretch the dough to the desired size on a pizza peel or lightly floured heat-resistant cutting board, taking care not to punch out all the air from the dough. Drizzle the dough with a bit of olive oil, then add some of the greens mixture, leaving a 1-inch border all around, and top with the Havarti and Parmesan. Using the back of a spoon, create 2 or 3 evenly spaced wells (Speed is key here, as the longer the dough sits, the harder it will be to slide into the oven.)

Slide the pizza onto the hot pizza stone or sheet pan and bake for 7 minutes. Meanwhile, crack 2 or 3 eggs into 2 or 3 ramekins or small bowls, depending on how many pizzas.

When the pizza has baked 7 minutes, slide 1 egg into each well and continue baking until the egg white is set, the cheese is melted, and the crust is browned and crisp, 5 to 7 minutes more.

Repeat the rolling, topping, and baking process with the remaining pizzas.

Season the pizzas with salt, black pepper, and pepper flakes as desired. Serve immediately with additional shaved Parmesan alongside.

Mushroom Toast
with Scrambled Eggs

Toast has a way of transcending any mealtime, as it's equally appropriate for breakfast, lunch, dinner, or even a snack. That's because it's always easy, comforting, and delicious. This toast takes it up a notch with filling scrambled eggs and earthy mushrooms. You might even call it sophisticated, but that doesn't make it any less perfect for when you need something yummy in a pinch. You can use any bread and any variety of mushrooms here—whatever you have handy, or whatever you like best!

SERVES 2

1 tablespoon extra-virgin olive oil

3 tablespoons unsalted butter

8 to 12 ounces mixed mushrooms, such as shiitake and cremini, sliced if the caps are larger than bite-size

1½ teaspoons kosher salt, plus more to taste

6 large eggs, beaten

3 ounces goat cheese

2 slices crusty bread, such as sourdough, toasted

Freshly ground black pepper

4 sprigs fresh thyme

In a large nonstick skillet, heat the olive oil and 1 tablespoon of the butter over medium heat. When the butter is melted and just bubbling, add the mushrooms, season with the salt, and increase the heat to high. Cook, stirring occasionally, until golden, about 8 minutes. Reduce the heat to medium and continue to cook until just caramelized and soft, 2 to 3 minutes more. Transfer the mushrooms to a plate.

Add the remaining 2 tablespoons butter to the skillet and melt over medium heat. Add the eggs and cook, using a spatula to move them around in the pan, letting the uncooked egg run underneath, to your desired doneness. Taste and add salt as needed.

Spread the goat cheese onto the toasts. Add the scrambled eggs, then the mushrooms. Season each piece with pepper and garnish with thyme.

Hearty Mixed Greens Quiche

It's a quiche party and all your favorite hearty greens are invited. Kale, Swiss chard, and spinach are always great guests, but this dish is also a wonderful chance to use up greens you might have left over from the tops of beet or carrot bunches (don't waste those!). For even more greenery, we like to serve it with a simple salad alongside for some crunch and acidity. We love making a flaky butter crust from scratch, but if you want to use store-bought pie crust we won't be mad. If you do go for it, double the recipe, shape the dough into two rounds, and freeze the extra one for up to a month. Let it sit on the counter for about 20 minutes before you roll it out and continue on to this quiche party.

SERVES 8 TO 10

2 tablespoons extra-virgin olive oil

1 bunch hearty greens, such as kale or Swiss chard, roughly chopped (about 4 cups)

Kosher salt

2 tablespoons unsalted butter

1 medium onion, halved and cut into ¼-inch-thick half-moons

Flaky Pie Dough (recipe follows)

⅓ to ½ cup freshly grated Parmesan cheese

2 tablespoons chopped fresh herbs, such as thyme or rosemary

2 cups whole milk

½ cup heavy cream

5 large eggs

¼ teaspoon ground nutmeg

Pinch of freshly ground black pepper

In a large skillet, heat the olive oil over medium heat. Add the greens and season with salt. Cook, stirring occasionally, until wilted, about 10 minutes. Transfer to a medium bowl.

Add the butter to the skillet and melt over medium heat. Add the onion and season with salt. Cook, stirring occasionally, until the onion is soft and translucent, about 5 minutes. Reduce the heat to low and continue cooking, stirring often, until the onion is tender and golden, 12 to 15 minutes more. Add the onion to the bowl with the greens.

CONTINUED

Position a rack in the center of the oven and preheat the oven to 375°F.

Unwrap the dough and place it on a lightly floured work surface. Roll out the dough to a round about 12 inches across and ¼ inch thick. Carefully transfer the dough to a 9-inch deep dish pie plate. Trim any excess. Place in the freezer to chill until firm, 15 to 20 minutes.

Line the pie shell with parchment paper or foil and add pie weights, uncooked rice, or dried beans. Bake for 30 minutes. Lift the parchment to remove the weights, return the crust to the oven, and bake until lightly golden, about 10 minutes more. Remove the crust and reduce the oven temperature to 350°F.

Place the pie plate on a sheet pan. Add the onion-greens mixture, followed by the Parmesan and chopped herbs.

In a large bowl, whisk together the milk, cream, eggs, 2 teaspoons salt, the nutmeg, and pepper. Slowly pour the egg mixture over the filling.

Bake until the crust is golden brown, the filling is set, and a small knife inserted into the center comes out clean, 45 minutes to 1 hour, rotating the sheet pan after 30 minutes.

Let cool slightly before slicing and serving.

Flaky Pie Dough

MAKES ENOUGH FOR ONE 9-INCH PIE

¾ cup all-purpose flour, plus more for dusting

¾ cup pastry flour

½ tablespoon kosher salt

10 tablespoons cold unsalted butter, cut into ½-inch cubes

¼ cup plus 2 tablespoons ice water

In a stand mixer, combine both flours and the salt. Place the bowl and the mixer's paddle attachment in the freezer to chill for 10 minutes.

Transfer half the flour mixture to a medium bowl. Add the butter to the remaining flour mixture and beat on low speed until combined. Scrape down the sides of the bowl and gradually add the remaining flour mixture while continuing to beat on low. Scrape down the sides of the bowl again. With the mixer running on low, slowly stream in the ice water just until the dough comes together and no dry streaks remain (you may not need all the water).

Turn the dough out onto a lightly floured surface and shape it into a 2-inch-thick disk. Wrap in plastic and refrigerate until firm, 30 minutes to 1 hour.

Eggs

Veggie Bowls

Rich in protein and perfect to prepare in advance of a busy week, this recipe is built to give you four made-ahead, easy weekday meals. The ingredients, which we recommend you store separately, will be good for four days covered in the fridge. Our method for boiling eggs here comes out perfect—Every. Single. Time. Take this 8-minute method with you to any dish. Or, if you prefer, the Soy-Marinated Eggs (page 72) are delicious on top, too.

SERVES 4

2 medium sweet potatoes, cut into ¼-inch-thick slices

2 tablespoons extra-virgin olive oil

Kosher salt and freshly ground black pepper

4 large eggs

2 bunches Tuscan kale, cut into thin strips

Juice of 1 lemon

1 cup Super Garlic Kimchi (page 251) or store-bought kimchi

2 large avocados, thinly sliced

Preheat the oven to 400°F. Line a sheet pan with parchment paper.

On the sheet pan, toss the sweet potatoes with 1 tablespoon of the olive oil and season with salt and pepper. Bake until tender and crisped around the edges, about 25 minutes. Let cool.

Meanwhile, set up a large bowl of ice and water. Bring a medium pot of water to a boil. Gently lower the eggs into the boiling water and cook for 8 minutes. Drain and immediately transfer to the ice bath. Let cool in the ice water for 10 minutes, then peel.

In a large bowl, combine the kale with the remaining 1 tablespoon olive oil and the lemon juice. Using your hands, massage the oil into the kale until the leaves are well coated and tender. Season with salt and pepper.

To assemble, layer the kale into bowls. Add the sweet potato rounds. Halve the eggs lengthwise and place 2 halves on top of each bowl. Season with salt and pepper. Add the kimchi and avocado. Serve.

Shrimp and Mushroom Scramble

Iri-tamago is Japan's take on scrambled eggs. Salty with a splash of soy sauce, sweet with a hint of mirin, and scrambled into tiny curds almost the size of rice, the comforting dish is a perfect addition to bento, sushi, or a simple bowl of rice. This scramble incorporates shiitake, shrimp, and cabbage, while taking inspiration from that classic with its seasoning and soft, delicate scrambled curds of egg in every bite. Shoyu, a Japanese-style soy sauce that's a 50/50 mix of soy and wheat, is widely available in grocery stores, but if you don't have it on hand, we recommend using soy sauce, which is 100 percent soy.

SERVES 2

4 large eggs

2 teaspoons shoyu

2 teaspoons mirin

1 tablespoon vegetable oil

½ pound large shrimp, peeled, deveined, and cut into ½-inch pieces

2 ounces shiitake mushrooms, thinly sliced

¼ cup thinly sliced cabbage

Kosher salt

4 tablespoons sliced scallions (about 4 scallions)

Steamed white rice, for serving

In a medium bowl, beat together the eggs, shoyu, and mirin.

In a large skillet, heat the oil over high heat. Add the shrimp and mushrooms and cook, undisturbed, until the shrimp are opaque and pink, 2 to 3 minutes. Add the cabbage and season with salt. Toss to combine and cook until the cabbage is slightly wilted, about 2 minutes more.

Add the egg mixture and 3 tablespoons of the scallions. Cook, stirring constantly, until the eggs are cooked to your desired consistency, 3 to 4 minutes.

Divide the rice between bowls and spoon the egg mixture over the top. Garnish with the remaining 1 tablespoon scallions and serve.

Spanish Tortilla

A signature dish in Spain, a Spanish tortilla is made using eggs and thinly sliced potatoes. The question of whether to use onion in a tortilla is hotly debated. The diehard purists, the sin cebollitas *(the "without onion-ers")* *insist that a true tortilla is eggs and potatoes. Nothing more, nothing less. The* cebollitas *(the "pro onion-ers") argue the contrary. You can decide for yourself, but we are* cebollitas—*and we think more is more. This recipe can be a great canvas for myriad add-ins or leftovers—Spanish peppers, tuna, or eggplant would be great additions. You can cook for longer if you want the eggs to set or leave them a little runny.*

**SERVES 6 TO 8
AS AN APPETIZER**

4 tablespoons extra-virgin olive oil

1 pound Yukon Gold potatoes, peeled and thinly sliced

1 medium yellow onion, diced

1½ teaspoons kosher salt

6 large eggs

In a 10-inch nonstick skillet, heat 2 tablespoons of the olive oil over high heat. Add the potatoes, reduce the heat to medium-low, and cook, stirring occasionally, until the potatoes are slightly softened, 7 to 10 minutes. Add the onion and 1 teaspoon of the salt. Cook, stirring occasionally, until the onion is translucent and the potatoes are tender, about 5 minutes more.

In a large bowl, beat the eggs and season with the remaining ½ teaspoon salt. Using a slotted spoon, transfer the potatoes and onion to the eggs and stir to combine. Drain the skillet and wipe it clean.

In the same skillet, heat the remaining 2 tablespoons olive oil over medium heat. Pour in the egg mixture and cook, stirring gently to keep the potatoes intact and creating large curds like scrambled eggs. As the edges set, pull them in to let the raw egg run underneath to the skillet's surface, continuing to stir in the center. Once the center is mostly set, 5 to 7 minutes, remove the skillet from the heat.

Cover the skillet with a large plate or upside-down baking sheet. Return the skillet to medium-low heat and carefully slide the now upside-down tortilla back into the skillet. Cook until the center is set and cooked through, 3 to 4 minutes.

Transfer to a serving plate and let cool for about 30 minutes. Slice into wedges and serve.

Breakfast Tacos

Breakfast tacos are always a crowd-pleaser. Corn tortillas piled high with scrambled eggs, refried beans, fresh salsa, and queso fresco . . . we can't think of a better way to start any day. And to be honest, we love these so much that sometimes we eat them for dinner. They're a bit unexpected for your usual Taco Tuesday, but we assure you: nobody will complain. This homemade salsa comes together in a flash, and it's the way to go if you want to truly take this favorite up a notch.

MAKES 12 TACOS

For the salsa

4 Roma (plum) tomatoes, diced

¼ cup chopped fresh cilantro

½ medium white onion, diced

1 teaspoon kosher salt, plus more to taste

Juice of 2 limes

For the tacos

12 (6-inch) corn tortillas

1 (16-ounce) can refried beans

12 large eggs

¼ cup whole milk

Kosher salt

1 tablespoon unsalted butter

¼ cup crumbled queso fresco

MAKE THE SALSA: In a medium bowl, toss together the tomatoes, cilantro, and onion. Stir in the salt and lime juice. Taste and adjust the seasoning as desired.

MAKE THE TACOS: Set a large skillet over medium-high heat. Working in batches add the tortillas and cook, flipping often, until puffy and lightly charred, 15 to 30 seconds per side. Stack the tortillas on a plate and cover with a kitchen towel to keep warm.

In the same skillet, warm the refried beans over low heat.

Meanwhile, in a large bowl, beat the eggs. Gradually pour in the milk while continuing to beat until smooth. Season with salt.

In a large nonstick skillet, melt the butter over low heat. Pour in the egg mixture and cook, stirring constantly with a silicone spatula, until the eggs are fluffy but still a bit loose, 3 to 4 minutes.

To assemble, spread some of the beans onto the tortillas. Add the eggs and a dollop of salsa. Sprinkle the queso fresco on top. Serve the tacos with the remaining salsa alongside.

Khai Jiao Thai Omelet

Seasoned with fish sauce and loaded with umami flavor, khai jiao *is somewhat like a cross between an omelet and a scrambled egg. The light caramelization the eggs get from shallow-frying makes it perfect for pairing with rice. Sriracha-style chili-garlic sauce is traditional on top, and ketchup is an excellent option if you're looking for a bit less heat. A seasoned wok is the traditional cookware for this recipe, as it adds a nice smoky edge to the* khai jiao, *but a stainless steel or nonstick skillet will also work (avoid using cast-iron as it has a tendency to overcook the eggs). This recipe is easy to scale up, but we don't advise cooking more than six eggs at a time.*

SERVES 2

3 large eggs, at room temperature

¾ teaspoon fish sauce

2 tablespoons thinly sliced scallions or garlic chives, plus more for serving (optional)

2 tablespoons vegetable oil

Sriracha, for serving (optional)

Ketchup, for serving (optional)

Cooked jasmine rice, for serving

In a small bowl, combine the eggs and the fish sauce. Holding a pair of chopsticks with one hand as if you were preparing to pick up a bite, dip the ends of the chopsticks into the egg mixture and use a brisk back-and-forth motion from one end of the bowl to the other to beat the eggs and fish sauce together until smooth. Stir in the scallions (if using) in the same manner.

In a large wok or skillet, heat the oil over medium heat. Pour in the egg mixture and cook, undisturbed, for 30 seconds, until the edges are just beginning to set. Use an offset spatula to gently lift the egg mixture on the side closest to you and push it toward the center of the skillet. Repeat on the far side. The uncooked egg will run onto the surface of the skillet as you push the cooked edges inward. Allow the egg to cook for a few seconds before you repeat this technique until the eggs are mostly set, but still a bit loose, another 30 seconds. Use the spatula to gently flip the khai jiao and continue to cook until the bottom surface is golden brown and the edges are caramelized, about 1 minute more. (If necessary to make flipping more manageable, you can break the khai jiao up into two pieces.)

Immediately transfer the khai jiao to a serving plate. If desired, drizzle with sriracha and/or ketchup. Serve with the rice alongside.

Savory Overnight Oats with Soy-Marinated Eggs

We love to let our oats soak up milk and yogurt overnight to make an extra creamy, no-cook base. And, news flash: Oatmeal does not always have to be sweet. Treat it as you would any other grain, and you'll quickly realize that oats' smooth, nutty flavor is very much up to the task of providing a base for jammy eggs, crunchy veggies, and garlic-chili oil that will knock your socks off. This favorite salty, spicy combination is just the beginning—after you fall in love with this dish, we dare you to try out other savory combinations, too.

SERVES 2

1 cup old-fashioned rolled oats

1¼ cups milk of your choice

½ cup plain yogurt of your choice

1 tablespoon chia seeds

1 tablespoon ground flaxseed

¼ teaspoon kosher salt

½ cup extra-virgin olive oil

6 garlic cloves, thinly sliced

1 Fresno or serrano chile, thinly sliced

2 teaspoons crushed red pepper flakes

For serving

2 Soy-Marinated Eggs (recipe follows)

Sautéed vegetables, such as spinach and mushrooms

Thinly sliced scallions, optional

Furikake

Flaky salt

In a medium bowl, stir together the oats, milk, yogurt, chia seeds, ground flaxseed, and salt. Divide between two bowls and refrigerate for at least 2 hours or preferably overnight.

Meanwhile, in a small saucepan, heat the olive oil over medium heat. Add the garlic, chile, and pepper flakes and cook, stirring constantly, until the garlic is golden brown and crisp, 2 to 3 minutes. Remove the pan from the heat and transfer the garlic-chile oil to a glass jar.

Before serving, heat the oat mixture in the microwave for 30 seconds to 1 minute to warm through. Serve the oats with desired toppings, drizzle with garlic-chile oil, sprinkle with furikake and flaky salt and serve.

CONTINUED

Soy-Marinated Eggs

MAKES 6 EGGS

6 large eggs

1 cup soy sauce

1 teaspoon kosher salt

1 teaspoon Chinese five-spice powder

1¼-inch piece fresh ginger, peeled and smashed

1 scallion, halved lengthwise

Star anise (optional)

Garlic cloves (optional)

Set up a large bowl of ice and water. Bring a large pot of water to a boil. Carefully lower the eggs into the boiling water. Cook, undisturbed, to your desired doneness: 5 to 6 minutes for a runny yolk, 7 to 8 minutes for a jammy yolk, or 9 to 10 minutes for a hard-boiled yolk. Drain the eggs and transfer them to the ice bath to cool completely, about 15 minutes.

Meanwhile, in a large saucepan, combine the soy sauce and 3 cups water and bring to a gentle simmer over medium heat. Add the salt, five-spice powder, ginger, scallion, and star anise and garlic, if using, and continue to simmer for 5 minutes. Turn off the heat.

Peel the eggs. In an airtight container, combine the peeled eggs and the marinade. Refrigerate for at least 8 hours, but preferably 2 days. Store refrigerated, in the marinade or drained, and eat within 4 days.

NOTE: Stir eggs during the first minute after placing in the boiling water, to help center the yolks. It's best to use a 2-quart saucepan for this—it will be a snug fit for the eggs, but you'll reduce water waste.

Scrambled Eggs with Crispy Pancetta

Bacon and eggs are an absolutely classic combination, but that doesn't mean they don't deserve a glow-up. Well, this dish is it. Pancetta is bacon's Italian cousin, and while it's not all that different, it's not quite the same either. Both come from pork belly and are cured, but bacon is smoked and sliced into strips, while pancetta is curled into a roll, then sliced or cubed. Either one you choose, this dish is both effortless, and elevated—words you don't always hear together. It will impress anyone lucky enough to share it with you.

SERVES 2

4 large eggs

Kosher salt and freshly ground black pepper

3 ounces cubed pancetta

2 tablespoons minced chives

In a large bowl, beat the eggs until smooth. Season with salt and pepper.

In a large nonstick skillet, cook the pancetta over medium heat, stirring occasionally, until the fat has rendered and the pancetta is crisp, 4 to 5 minutes. Using a slotted spoon, transfer the pancetta to a plate lined with paper towels, reserving the fat in the pan.

Add the eggs to the skillet over medium heat and use a silicone spatula to gently fold in the edges to create soft curds. Continue gently pushing and folding, pausing occasionally to allow the liquid eggs to form curds, 2 to 3 minutes total.

Transfer the eggs to a plate and top with the pancetta, chives, and additional salt and pepper as desired.

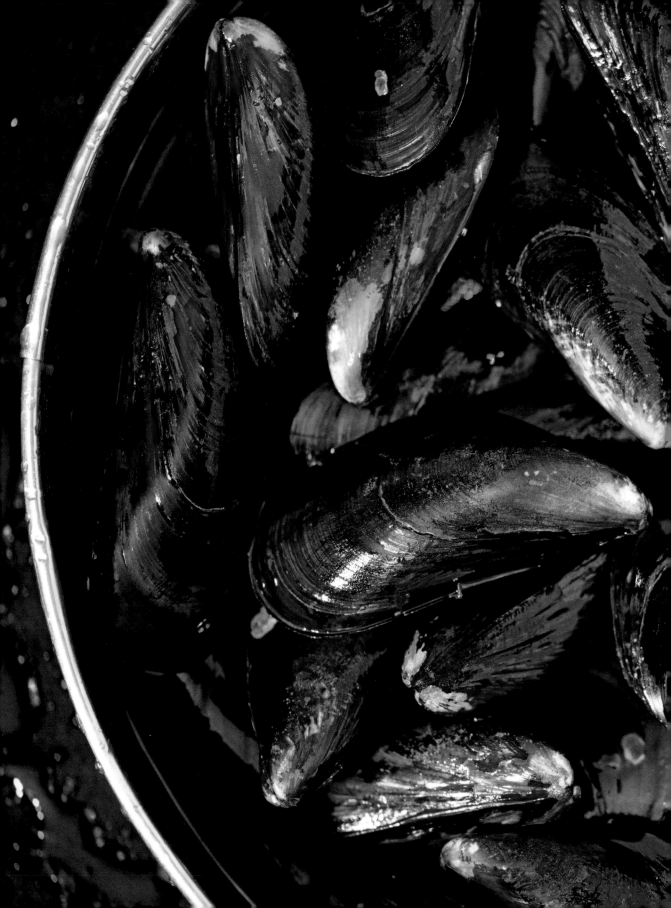

Fish and Shellfish

Pot o' Mussels

When you need an easy-to-make dinner for a group of friends who are down to share, look no further than this heaping pot of fun. Simmering the mussels in white wine couldn't be simpler, plus the whole dish requires just a handful of ingredients! We always pick farmed mussels over wild, as they're cleaner. For a super fast cleanup—and a rustic presentation—you can even serve the mussels at the table straight from the pot. Just be sure to add an empty bowl, too, for those shells. It's the perfect communal dish over which to break some bread—and we mean that literally, because you and your dinner mates will want plenty of the good, crusty kind for soaking up that irresistibly garlicky broth!

SERVES 4 TO 6

3 tablespoons extra-virgin olive oil

1 large yellow onion, chopped

4 garlic cloves, smashed

1 large tomato, chopped

½ cup dry white wine, such as Pinot Grigio or Sauvignon Blanc

1 cup Fish Stock (page 87) or white wine

4 pounds mussels, scrubbed and debearded (see Note)

Sliced crusty bread, for serving

Salted butter, for serving

In a Dutch oven, heat the olive oil over medium heat. Add the onion and cook, stirring occasionally, until beginning to soften, about 7 minutes. Add the garlic and tomato and cook until the garlic is fragrant, 1 minute more.

Add the wine, fish stock, and mussels. Cover, increase the heat to high, and cook, shaking the pot frequently, until the mussels have opened, 8 to 10 minutes. Discard any that do not open.

Serve the mussels straight from the pot with the bread and salted butter alongside.

NOTE: To scrub the mussels, let them sit in a pot of cold water for at least 30 minutes. Using a stiff scrubbing brush, wash the mussels, and discard any with broken shells. Pull or scrape off the "beard" from each and rinse again.

Blackened Salmon

Salmon is widely beloved, and one of the easiest ways to prepare it is to load it up with tasty seasonings. We like to work this seasoning mixture into as fine a texture as possible—basically until it's flavor dust—so it sticks to the fish. A quick pan sear before a roast in the oven is what gives the fish its nice, blackened crust.

SERVES 3 OR 4

2 teaspoons kosher salt

2 teaspoons smoked paprika

2 teaspoons ground coriander

1 teaspoon dried basil

1 teaspoon dried thyme

1 teaspoon freshly ground black pepper

½ teaspoon garlic powder

1 pound skin-on salmon fillet

2 tablespoons neutral oil

Lemon wedges, for serving

Preheat the oven to 350°F.

Using a spice grinder, mortar and pestle, or a sharp knife and a cutting board, grind or finely break down the salt, smoked paprika, coriander, basil, thyme, pepper, and garlic powder. Season the salmon with the spice and herb mixture, pressing to adhere.

Heat a grill pan or cast-iron skillet over medium-high heat. Brush the pan with the oil and add the fish skin-side down. Cook, undisturbed, until the salmon is opaque (light pink) partway up its side from the bottom and the skin lifts easily from the pan, 1 to 2 minutes. Flip the salmon over and continue to cook until completely opaque and nicely charred, about 3 minutes more. Flip the salmon once more so that it's skin-side down.

Transfer the salmon to the oven and roast until an instant-read thermometer inserted in the center registers 140°F, 6 to 8 minutes. Remove the salmon from the oven, cover, and let rest until the temperature reaches 145°F, about 10 minutes longer.

Serve with lemon wedges for squeezing.

Pan-Fried Red Snapper

Dredged in a light batter and quickly pan-fried, this red snapper is easy to cook on a weeknight but is tasty enough to feel decadent any day. Briefly brining the fish before cooking gives the final dish an automatic boost, with a moisture and flakiness that can't be beat. It helps achieve even cooking, even seasoning, and even more delicious flavor. We love adding coriander and cumin to the batter before frying, but feel free to mix it up with any spices you wish. Garnish with extra sesame seeds or a dry condiment like seaweed gomashio *(sesame and salt), which is similar to* furikake.

SERVES 2

1 tablespoon plus 1 teaspoon kosher salt

Juice of 1 lemon

1 pound red snapper fillet, cut into 2-inch pieces

⅓ cup potato starch

1 teaspoon ground coriander

1 teaspoon ground cumin

1 large egg

2 to 3 tablespoons neutral oil

2 tablespoons soy sauce

1 tablespoon rice vinegar

½-inch piece fresh ginger, peeled and thinly sliced

1 scallion, thinly sliced

Gomashio or sesame seeds, for serving

Steamed rice, for serving

In a large bowl, combine 1 tablespoon of the salt, the lemon juice, and 2 cups water and stir to dissolve the salt. Add the fish to the brine and let sit for 20 minutes. Drain the fish and spread on a wire rack to dry, about 10 minutes.

Preheat the oven to 200°F. Line a baking sheet with parchment paper.

In a shallow bowl, stir together the potato starch, coriander, cumin, and remaining 1 teaspoon salt. In a separate shallow bowl, beat the egg.

In a large cast-iron skillet, heat the oil over medium-high heat. Working in batches, dip the fish into the dry mixture, pressing to adhere, then into the egg, allowing any excess to drip off. Add the coated fish to the skillet and cook until crisp and golden brown, 3 to 4 minutes per side.

Transfer the fish to the prepared baking sheet and keep warm in the oven while you repeat with the remaining fish.

In a small bowl, whisk together the soy sauce, rice vinegar, ginger, and scallion.

Divide the fish between two plates and garnish with gomashio. Serve with rice and the sauce alongside for dipping.

Poached Mahi Mahi in Tomato Sauce

You probably pour yourself a nice glass of chilled white wine when you're eating fish, but are you grabbing for that bottle when you're cooking it, too? If not, you should be. In this recipe, along with sweet roasted tomatoes, it acts as the first layer in building a rich, creamy sauce. Mahi mahi, light in taste but firm in texture, takes on the flavor beautifully and holds up well as it cooks in the liquid, though halibut, swordfish, or tuna would be great, too. We think it's well worth making your own fish stock here— minimal effort, maximum umami-richness to punch up sauces, stock, and stews. (Plus, you can keep it in your freezer. If you store it in an ice cube tray, you'll be able to thaw a little bit whenever you need it.) Consult your local fishmonger to get what you need, or just use water in its place.

SERVES 4

2 tablespoons extra-virgin olive oil

1 pint cherry tomatoes

3 garlic cloves, minced

2 tablespoons minced shallot or scallions

Kosher salt and freshly ground black pepper

¼ cup dry white wine, such as Pinot Grigio or Sauvignon Blanc

1 bay leaf

4 mahi mahi fillets (6 ounces each)

4 tablespoons (½ stick) unsalted butter, at room temperature

1½ cups Fish Stock (recipe follows)

2½ tablespoons all-purpose flour

½ cup heavy cream, plus more as needed

1 tablespoon fresh lemon juice

Fresh thyme leaves, for garnish (optional)

Position a rack in the lower third of the oven and preheat the oven to 350°F.

In a large ovenproof skillet, heat the olive oil over medium heat. Add the cherry tomatoes, garlic, and 1 tablespoon of the shallot and season with salt and pepper. Cook, stirring often, until the tomatoes are soft and beginning to burst, 6 to 8 minutes.

Using a wooden spoon, crush the tomatoes against the side of the skillet. Pour in the white wine and scrape up any browned bits from the bottom of the pan. Add the bay leaf.

Season the fish with salt and pepper. Add the fillets to the skillet in an even layer. Dividing evenly, sprinkle the fish with the remaining 1 tablespoon shallot and 1 tablespoon of the butter. Pour in the fish stock and enough water to barely cover the fish and bring to a simmer. Place a sheet of parchment paper over the fish.

Transfer the skillet to the oven and roast until the fish is opaque and flaky, 8 to 12 minutes. Remove the parchment paper and transfer the fish to a serving platter.

Return the skillet to medium-high heat and bring the liquid to a boil. Cook for 5 minutes to reduce by about half.

Meanwhile, in a small bowl, combine the remaining 3 tablespoons butter and the flour and stir to form a paste.

When the sauce is reduced, stir in the butter-flour paste to dissolve. Add the cream. Return the mixture to a boil and cook until the sauce is thick enough to coat the back of a spoon. If the sauce seems too thick, add more cream, about 1 tablespoon at a time, to thin it out. Taste and season with the lemon juice and more salt and pepper as needed.

Spoon the sauce over the fish and garnish with thyme, if using. Serve immediately.

CONTINUED

Fish Stock

MAKES 2 QUARTS

2 pounds fish bones and/or heads

2 large yellow onions, quartered

8 to 10 sprigs fresh parsley

1 cup dry white wine, such as Pinot Grigio or Sauvignon Blanc

1 teaspoon fresh lemon juice

¼ teaspoon kosher salt

In a stockpot or Dutch oven, combine the fish bones, onions, parsley, wine, lemon juice, and salt. Add 3 quarts water to cover everything and bring to a simmer over medium heat. Continue to simmer, occasionally skimming the surface, until the broth is fragrant and richly flavored, about 1 hour.

Strain the stock, discarding the solids. Let cool and transfer to an airtight container. Store refrigerated for up to 4 days or frozen for up to 6 months.

Fish Pakora

Fish pakora is a traditional homestyle Punjabi recipe, and a staple appetizer frequently served at celebratory events like weddings and birthday parties. Crispy and light thanks to a coating of besan *(chickpea flour) before frying, these fritters get their flavor from an array of bright Indian spices that are complemented perfectly by a mint-yogurt chutney. Vivid color, imparted by red or orange food coloring in the marinade, makes the dish instantly recognizable, but it's just as delicious without. If you can't find fenugreek leaves, try celery leaves or just a small pinch (too much can be bitter) of ground fenugreek.*

SERVES 4

For the fish

2 tablespoons vegetable oil

1 tablespoon ground coriander

1 tablespoon garam masala

½ teaspoon ground cumin

½ teaspoon ground ginger

½ teaspoon onion powder

½ teaspoon crushed red pepper flakes

½ teaspoon paprika

½ teaspoon ground turmeric

½ teaspoon fenugreek leaves

½ teaspoon kosher salt

½ teaspoon freshly ground black pepper

1 pound white fish fillets, such as cod, cut into bite-size pieces

2 teaspoons grated garlic

1 serrano chile, diced

For the mint chutney

1 bunch fresh mint, stems removed

¼ cup plain yogurt

½ teaspoon kosher salt

For assembly

Vegetable oil, for frying

1½ cups chickpea flour

Lemon wedges, for serving

MARINATE THE FISH: In a resealable zip-top bag or large bowl, combine the oil, coriander, garam masala, cumin, ginger, onion powder, pepper flakes, paprika, turmeric, fenugreek, salt, and black pepper. Add the fish, garlic, and chile and toss to coat well. Refrigerate for 30 minutes to 1 hour.

MEANWHILE, MAKE THE CHUTNEY: In a food processor, combine the mint, yogurt, salt, and 1 tablespoon water. Process about 1 minute, scraping down the sides as needed, until the mint is thoroughly chopped and the sauce is smooth. Add more water, 1 teaspoon at a time, as needed if the chutney seems too thick.

TO ASSEMBLE: Pour 2 inches oil into a deep, heavy-bottomed skillet. Clip a thermometer to the side and heat over medium-high heat to 350°F.

Place the chickpea flour in a shallow bowl. Remove the fish from the marinade and toss in the chickpea flour to coat. Shake off any excess. Working in batches, carefully add the fish to the hot oil and cook, making sure the fish is submerged, until crisp and golden, 2 to 3 minutes per side. Transfer the fish to a plate lined with paper towels.

Arrange the pakoras on a serving platter and squeeze lemon over the top. Serve immediately with the mint chutney alongside.

Baked Salmon with Olives

Jammy tomatoes, salty green olives, and garlicky bread crumbs combine to bring you a saucy, briny hunk of salmon, just how we like it. If that wasn't enough to convince you, you should know this dish comes together in less than 15 minutes. It's vying for a place in your weeknight repertoire, and we think it deserves one.

SERVES 4

2 slices day-old French bread, roughly torn

2 garlic cloves, smashed

½ cup plus 1 tablespoon extra-virgin olive oil

4 Roma (plum) tomatoes, halved and crushed by hand

10 pitted green olives, smashed

1 small red onion, chopped

1 teaspoon dried oregano

1 to 1½ pounds skin-on salmon fillet, cut into 4 pieces

Kosher salt

Preheat the oven to 350°F.

In a food processor, pulse the bread into coarse crumbs. Add the garlic and 1 tablespoon of the olive oil and pulse again.

Pour the remaining ½ cup olive oil into a 9 × 13-inch baking dish. Layer the tomatoes, olives, onion, and oregano. Place the fillets on top and sprinkle with the bread crumbs and season with salt.

Bake the salmon until the bread crumb topping is golden brown and the salmon is opaque and flakes easily with a fork, 6 to 8 minutes.

Serve family-style.

Seared Ahi Tuna Sandwiches with Wasabi-Ginger Mayo

Wasabi is a delicious and often forgotten condiment that, when combined with mayonnaise, can take a sandwich from basic lunchtime staple to something that is truly succulent and spicy and tangy. The crunch of homemade pickles elevate this one step closer to sandwich stardom. Beyond lunch, these sandwiches are perfect for an outdoor summer dinner with a salad or fries on the side that will make you feel like you're on a beachy vacation even if you aren't.

SERVES 4

For the tuna

¼ cup mayonnaise

4 teaspoons soy sauce

2 teaspoons sesame oil

1 garlic clove, minced

½ teaspoon grated fresh ginger

Freshly ground black pepper

1 to 1½ pounds ahi tuna steaks

For the wasabi-ginger mayo

⅓ cup mayonnaise

1 teaspoon wasabi paste

1 teaspoon grated fresh ginger

For assembly

2 tablespoons unsalted butter

4 brioche buns, split

4 to 8 large lettuce leaves, such as green-leaf, Boston, or Bibb

Refrigerator Pickles (page 260) or store-bought pickles

Lemon wedges, for serving

MARINATE THE TUNA: In a resealable zip-top bag or large bowl, whisk together the mayonnaise, soy sauce, sesame oil, garlic, ginger, and pepper until smooth. Add the tuna and turn to coat. Marinate for at least 30 minutes at room temperature or up to 2 hours in the refrigerator.

MEANWHILE, MAKE THE WASABI-GINGER MAYO: In a small bowl, whisk together the mayonnaise, wasabi, and ginger until smooth. Cover and refrigerate until ready to use.

Remove the tuna from the marinade. Heat a large skillet over medium-high heat. Add the tuna and cook, flipping halfway through, until a deeply browned crust forms, 3 to 4 minutes total. Transfer the tuna to a cutting board to rest.

TO ASSEMBLE: In the same skillet, melt the butter over medium-high heat. Add the buns cut-sides down and cook until toasted and golden brown, 1 to 2 minutes each. Transfer the buns to a plate.

Cut each tuna steak into ¼-inch-thick slices. Spread a generous amount of the wasabi-ginger mayo on the insides of each bun. Add a layer of lettuce to each bottom bun, then the sliced tuna, with the pieces overlapping slightly. Add pickles and finish with the bun tops. Serve immediately with the lemon wedges alongside.

Curry Shrimp

Flavorful and easy to make, this shrimp dish has roots in Jamaica. The fast-cooking seafood gets tossed with curry powder, which gives this favorite of ours perfect spice and beautiful color. Add some bell peppers and cook them to crisp-tenderness, serve over rice, and you have a complete and filling meal that comes together with ease.

SERVES 4

1 pound large shrimp, peeled and deveined

½ teaspoon kosher salt, plus more to taste

½ teaspoon freshly ground black pepper, plus more to taste

2 teaspoons curry powder

2 tablespoons vegetable oil

½ green bell pepper, thinly sliced

½ red bell pepper, thinly sliced

1 small yellow onion, diced

3 garlic cloves, minced

Fresh thyme sprigs

3 cups cooked rice, for serving

In a resealable zip-top bag or medium bowl, toss the shrimp with the salt, pepper, and ½ teaspoon of the curry powder to coat. Refrigerate for 30 minutes to 1 hour.

In a wok or large skillet, heat the oil over medium-high heat. Add the bell peppers, onion, and garlic and cook, stirring occasionally, until the onion is soft and translucent, about 5 minutes.

Reduce the heat to medium. Add the shrimp, thyme, and the remaining 1½ teaspoons curry powder and cook, stirring occasionally, until the shrimp is opaque and pink, about 5 minutes. Season with additional salt and pepper to taste.

Serve on top of rice.

Trout Amandine

Trout amandine is a classic, old-school recipe that never goes out of style. It's as easy to pull off as any other sautéed fish dish, but we think it's even better thanks to toasted almonds and a divine butter sauce that you'll want to live in like a cozy winter sweater. Serve this dish with rice or plenty of crusty French bread to soak up those luxurious pools of butter, along with a green vegetable like asparagus or peas that will match the delicate flavor of the trout.

SERVES 4

4 trout fillets (5 ounces each)

2 teaspoons garlic powder

Kosher salt and freshly ground black pepper

1 cup sliced almonds

1 cup plus 2 tablespoons all-purpose flour

2 large eggs

½ cup vegetable oil

2 tablespoons unsalted butter

1 cup whole milk

Juice of 1 lemon, plus lemon slices for serving

1 tablespoon chopped fresh thyme, plus more for serving

Flaky salt, for serving

Pat the trout fillets dry. Season with the garlic powder and kosher salt and pepper to taste.

In a medium skillet, toast the almonds over medium heat, stirring constantly, until fragrant and lightly golden, 2 to 3 minutes. Transfer ¼ cup of the almonds to a small bowl and the remainder to a food processor.

Add 1 cup of the flour to the food processor and process until the almonds are coarsely ground and no large pieces remain, about 1 minute. Transfer to a shallow bowl. In a separate shallow bowl, beat the eggs.

Working with one fillet at a time, dip the trout in the beaten egg, allowing any excess to drip off. Dredge through the flour mixture, pressing to adhere.

CONTINUED

In a large skillet, heat ¼ cup of the oil over medium heat. Add 2 fillets and cook until golden brown, 3 to 5 minutes per side. Transfer the fillets to a serving platter. Add the remaining ¼ cup oil and repeat with the remaining 2 fillets.

Wipe out the skillet. Add the butter and melt over medium heat. Whisk in the remaining 2 tablespoons flour and simmer until the flour has thickened and toasted slightly, 2 to 3 minutes. Whisk in the milk and simmer until the sauce is thick enough to coat the back of a spoon, 2 to 3 minutes more. Whisk in the lemon juice, thyme, and kosher salt and pepper to taste and cook until the thyme is fragrant, about 1 minute more.

Spoon the sauce over the fillets. Garnish with the reserved toasted almonds, more thyme, and flaky salt. Top with the lemon slices and serve.

Salmon Turnovers with Spicy Relish

These turnovers are inspired by Belizean panades *(that country's answer to the empanada), which are traditionally stuffed with fish (often tuna), chicken, or beans and use corn masa tortillas. Our version highlights salmon, veering slightly from the classic. No matter what goes inside, they're delectable filled pastries served with a knock-your-socks-off habanero pepper relish. If you have a tortilla press, you're going to want to use it here, but if not, no worries. We dare you to eat just one.*

MAKES 12 TURNOVERS

For the relish

½ cup minced white onion

1 habanero pepper, seeded and minced

1 teaspoon kosher salt

¼ cup distilled white vinegar

Cilantro leaves, for garnish

For the filling

1 tablespoon vegetable oil

1 (1-pound) salmon fillet

½ medium white onion, grated

1 (1.41-ounce) packet sazón (see Note)

Kosher salt

For the masa

2 cups masa harina

1 (1.41-ounce) packet sazón

Vegetable oil, for frying

MAKE THE RELISH: In a small bowl, stir together the onion, habanero, salt, vinegar, and ¼ cup water. Refrigerate until ready to use.

MAKE THE FILLING: In a large skillet, heat the oil over medium heat. Add the salmon, onion, sazón, and salt. Cook until the salmon has flaked and fallen apart into small pieces, 5 to 7 minutes. Remove the skillet from the heat.

MAKE THE MASA: In a medium bowl, combine 1 cup water, the masa, and sazón and stir until well incorporated into a sandy dough. Continue to add water, 1 tablespoon at a time, and mix until the dough is in a cohesive mound that is easy to knead, but not tacky. Cover the dough with a damp kitchen towel for 5 minutes.

Fish and Shellfish

CONTINUED

Divide the dough into 12 equal balls. Line a tortilla press with parchment paper or plastic wrap. Working with one at a time, press each ball of dough into a flat tortilla. (Alternatively, working with one at a time, lay the balls of dough between two sheets of parchment paper. Using a large baking dish, apply slow and even pressure to flatten.)

Pour 2 inches oil into a large, heavy-bottomed pot. Clip a thermometer to the side and heat over medium-high heat to 350°F.

Meanwhile, place a spoonful of the filling in the center of each tortilla. Fold the dough in half over the filling and press the edges together with a fork to seal. Working in batches, carefully add the turnovers to the oil and cook until deeply golden and bubbling on the surface, 2 to 3 minutes. Transfer to a plate lined with paper towels. Repeat with the remaining turnovers.

Serve the turnovers with the relish and garnish with cilantro.

NOTE: Most grocery stores carry sazón in the Mexican or Latin aisle. The word *sazón* just means "seasoning," so be sure to read the package carefully for the correct spice blend—in this case, culantro y achiote. Culantro is similar to cilantro, though some folks say it tastes less "soapy." It's often used in cooking (and a lot of Caribbean cooking), while the more delicate cilantro is frequently used as a garnish. If you can't find this super flavorful blend, opt for achiote powder.

Oyster Stuffing

Sure, any kind of stuffing is decadent and delicious, with its dense nuggets of bread, aromatic herbs, and (often) sausage—but why settle for level 1? This stuffing (or "dressing," if you want to be technical, since it doesn't cook inside *a bird) goes beyond the realm of ordinary Thanksgiving sides. With hot Italian sausage plus briny oysters, it delivers savory, rich, umami earthiness brightened by tart green apple. Using good-quality bakery bread here goes the extra mile, as you want it to soak up the flavor without falling apart.*

SERVES 6 TO 8

Softened butter, for greasing

1 pound hot Italian sausage, casings removed

1 (1-pound) loaf day-old bread, such as baguette or ciabatta, torn (about 10 cups)

1 cup diced celery

1 large yellow onion, diced

2 tart apples, such as Granny Smith, diced

1 (1-pint) jar shucked raw oysters, drained and chopped

2 sticks (8 ounces) unsalted butter, melted

2 cups chopped mushrooms

2 teaspoons herbes de Provence

Kosher salt and freshly ground black pepper

½ cup chicken stock

Preheat the oven to 350°F. Grease a 9 × 13-inch baking dish.

In a medium skillet, cook the sausage over medium-high heat until browned and cooked through, about 5 minutes. Using a slotted spoon, transfer the sausage to a large bowl.

Arrange the bread on a baking sheet and bake until lightly toasted, about 5 minutes. Add the bread to the bowl with the sausage. Leave the oven on.

Add the celery, onion, apples, oysters, melted butter, mushrooms, and herbes de Provence and toss to combine well. Season generously with salt and pepper. Pour in the stock and stir to coat. Transfer the stuffing to the prepared baking dish, pressing down to fit as needed.

Cover with foil and bake until the bread is puffed and the stuffing is fragrant, about 20 minutes. Uncover and continue baking until the top of the stuffing is crisp and lightly browned, about 15 minutes more. Serve.

Poultry and Pork

Cast-Iron Chicken Thighs with Crispy Kale

Skin-on chicken in a cast-iron skillet is an absolute classic—there's just something about the way that skin comes out perfectly crispy, every single time. This dish is straightforward with a protein and a green, and you can feel free to dress it up, down, and all around any way you like, based on what's in your fridge when the mood strikes. We love the way sturdy kale holds up in the oven—in fact, you don't even need to remove the thick ribs here, as they add a nice crunch to the finished dish. Serve this over any grain for a well-rounded meal, and if you are down with dairy, go for the dollop of yogurt on top for a nice contrast of texture.

SERVES 4

4 bone-in, skin-on chicken thighs

Kosher salt and freshly ground black pepper

¼ cup extra-virgin olive oil

1 bunch kale, roughly chopped

1 head garlic, separated into cloves, smashed, and peeled

3 shallots, thinly sliced

½ to 1 teaspoon crushed red pepper flakes

Fresh lemon juice

Chopped fresh cilantro or chives, for serving (optional)

Plain whole-milk Greek yogurt or crème fraîche, for serving (optional)

Preheat the oven to 450°F.

Season the chicken generously with salt and pepper.

In a cast-iron skillet, heat the olive oil over medium-high heat. When the oil is shimmering, add the chicken, skin-side down, and cook, undisturbed, until the skin is crispy and browned, about 10 minutes.

Flip the chicken thighs over. Add the kale to the skillet, arranging it around the chicken. Nestle in the garlic cloves and shallots. Sprinkle everything with the pepper flakes.

Transfer to the oven and roast until the kale is crispy and the juices in the thickest part of the chicken run clear, about 20 minutes and registers at least 165°F.

Squeeze fresh lemon juice over the chicken. If desired, top with cilantro and Greek yogurt.

Panko-Fried Chicken Tenders

Katsu, *a popular deep-fried dish in Japan, is a protein cutlet (usually pork or chicken) coated in panko and fried to perfection. It is most often served with curry, on skewers, or as part of a bento box with delicious little sides. Here, we take inspiration from that dish with chicken tenders and an at-home frying process. Once the chicken is moist on the inside and crispy on the outside, load up your plate with rice, nori, pickles, and burdock for a variety of textures and flavors in every bite. Don't miss the tonkatsu sauce, a sweet and savory dipping sauce that takes every crunch to the next level.*

SERVES 3 OR 4

For the chicken

1½ pounds chicken tenders

Kosher salt and freshly ground black pepper

Canola oil, for deep-frying

½ cup all-purpose flour

3 large eggs

2 cups panko bread crumbs

For the tonkatsu sauce

¼ cup ketchup

¼ cup Worcestershire sauce

1 tablespoon soy sauce

1 teaspoon sugar

For serving (optional)

Salted roasted nori

Cooked sushi rice

Refrigerator Pickles (page 260)

Sesame seeds

MAKE THE CHICKEN: Pat the chicken dry with paper towels. Generously season all over with salt and pepper.

Pour 2 inches oil into a Dutch oven. Clip a thermometer to the side of the pot and heat the oil to 350°F.

Meanwhile, place the flour in a shallow bowl. In a second shallow bowl, beat the eggs with 1 tablespoon water. Place the panko in a third shallow bowl.

Working with 2 to 3 chicken tenders at a time, dip them into flour and turn to coat, shaking off any excess. Dip them in the egg wash, allowing any excess egg to drip off. Dredge them through the panko, pressing to adhere evenly. Repeat with the remaining chicken.

Working in batches (to avoid crowding the pot), add the chicken to the oil and cook for 2 to 3 minutes. Flip and cook until the crust is golden brown all over, 2 to 3 minutes more. Transfer to a plate lined with paper towels to drain. Repeat with the remaining chicken, allowing the oil to return to 350°F between batches.

MEANWHILE, MAKE THE TONKATSU SAUCE: In a small bowl, whisk together the ketchup, Worcestershire sauce, soy sauce, and sugar.

To serve, slice the chicken tenders on a diagonal and arrange them in the center of a platter. Serve with the tonkatsu sauce. If desired, surround the chicken with small bowls or piles of nori, rice, pickles, and sesame seeds.

Citrus-Marinated Chicken

When winter is at its bitterest and coldest, citrus always comes through as the bright spot. We especially love tangerines, as they'll give you that classic pucker, but are still subtly sweet. Here, they brighten up oven-roasted chicken thighs, infusing them with a marinade that's super easy to throw together. And, for the record, this dish is amazing any time of year—just use oranges in place of the tangerines if they're not in season. Serve this with any roasted veggie and/or grain you like, as it goes well with pretty much anything.

SERVES 4

2 pounds boneless, skinless chicken thighs

Grated zest of 1 tangerine

Juice of 2 tangerines

Grated zest and juice of 1 lemon

1 tablespoon extra-virgin olive oil

4 garlic cloves, roughly chopped

¼ cup thinly sliced red onion

2 scallions, halved crosswise

¼ cup chopped fresh parsley

2 tablespoons kosher salt

2 teaspoons freshly ground black pepper

In a resealable zip-top bag or large bowl, combine the chicken, tangerine zest, tangerine juice, lemon zest, lemon juice, olive oil, garlic, red onion, scallions, parsley, salt, and pepper. Massage to coat the chicken. Marinate at room temperature for at least 2 hours or refrigerated overnight.

Preheat the oven to 450°F.

Transfer the chicken to a large baking dish or a cast-iron skillet and pour in the marinade. Roast until an instant-read thermometer registers 165°F, about 35 minutes, spooning the sauce over the chicken halfway through.

Serve family-style.

Pork Meatballs with Fresh Ginger

These meatballs are adapted from a classic recipe in Chinese cooking known as Lion's Head. A signature of Huaiyang cuisine, one of the four major cuisines in China (alongside Cantonese, Shandong, and Sichuan), it got its name from the meatballs' resemblance to the Chinese guardian lion. Usually served as a celebratory dish in banquet-style meals, the meatballs are high in flavor and elevate any evening. Those meatballs are made with ground pork, ginger, and minced shiitake mushrooms, then wrapped in cabbage leaves and steamed. A meatball tip you can take with you: If the mixture is sticking to your hands, keep a small bowl of water next to you and dip your fingers as needed, or rub your palms with oil. When you cook the meatballs, the oil in the pan will spatter slightly, so be careful and work quickly—use a splatter guard if you have one handy.

SERVES 8

1½ teaspoons cornstarch

1 tablespoon plus 2 teaspoons soy sauce

1½ to 2 pounds napa cabbage

1 pound ground pork

1 teaspoon rice wine

½ teaspoon sesame oil

1 teaspoon minced fresh ginger

1 teaspoon chopped scallion, plus more for serving

1 cup water chestnuts, chopped

1 large egg

1½ teaspoons kosher salt

½ teaspoon freshly ground black pepper

¼ cup vegetable oil

Steamed rice, for serving

In a small bowl, combine the cornstarch with 2 teaspoons of the soy sauce and 2 teaspoons water and stir until smooth.

Trim the stem from the base of the cabbage. Remove the 4 outer leaves and set aside. Cut the cabbage lengthwise, through the base, going about halfway up toward the tip of the leaves, then pull the two halves apart with your hands. Chop the leafy part of the cabbage into 2-inch segments. Slice the dense core into narrow wedges.

CONTINUED

In a large bowl, combine the pork, rice wine, sesame oil, ginger, scallion, water chestnuts, egg, 1 teaspoon of the salt, and the pepper. Use your hands to mix in a clockwise motion until homogenous and well combined. Add 2 tablespoons water and mix again to incorporate. Repeat with an additional 2 tablespoons water. Add the cornstarch mixture and mix again.

Divide the meat into 4 equal portions, then divide each portion in half. Using your hands, roll each portion into a ball, wetting your hands as needed.

In a large, deep skillet, heat the vegetable oil over medium-high heat. Carefully lower the meatballs into the hot oil. Cook, turning as soon as they appear golden brown on the bottom, 2 to 3 minutes. Continue to cook until browned all over, about 3 minutes more. Transfer the meatballs to a plate lined with paper towels.

Reduce the heat to medium and add the chopped cabbage to the skillet. Pour in 1 cup water and cook, stirring occasionally, until the cabbage is wilted, 3 to 5 minutes.

Arrange the meatballs on top of the cabbage in the skillet, spacing them apart. Place the 4 reserved cabbage leaves on top, overlapping them slightly to create a canopy over the meatballs. Sprinkle with the remaining ½ teaspoon salt and drizzle with the remaining 1 tablespoon soy sauce. Cover and simmer until the meatballs are cooked through, 20 to 25 minutes.

Arrange the cabbage and meatballs on a serving platter. Sprinkle with the additional scallion and serve with steamed rice alongside.

Grilled Chicken with Plantain Chips and Cabbage Slaw

Juicy grilled chicken, rich plantain chips, and crisp cabbage salad are an unstoppable trio, and we're here to tell you they should be part of your new favorite dinner lineup. This recipe tips its hat to pollo chuco *from Honduras, known for being high on flavor and easy on your wallet. It's one of the most popular dishes there, especially along the northern coast, a hub of plantain production, and it's become well loved, served both in homes and at restaurants. The sauce here is a variation on* aderezo, *which is a condiment in Central America.*

SERVES 4

For the chicken

4 boneless, skinless chicken breasts (about 2 pounds)

1 teaspoon ground cumin

1 teaspoon garlic powder

½ teaspoon ground sage

½ teaspoon dried oregano

½ teaspoon bay leaf powder

½ teaspoon freshly ground black pepper

2 tablespoons distilled white vinegar

1 tablespoon extra-virgin olive oil

For the cabbage slaw

3 cups thinly sliced green cabbage

½ cup thinly sliced red onion

Juice of 1 lemon

For the sauce

½ cup mayonnaise

¼ cup ketchup

2 tablespoons yellow mustard

1 teaspoon garlic powder

¼ cup cilantro, finely chopped

For assembly

Canola oil, for greasing and for frying

3 green plantains, ends trimmed and peeled

Kosher salt

MARINATE THE CHICKEN: Halve the chicken breasts crosswise, if thick. Place the chicken breasts in a resealable zip-top bag or between two sheets of parchment paper. Use a rolling pin or a meat tenderizer to pound the chicken breasts to a ½-inch thickness.

CONTINUED

In the same bag or a large bowl, combine the chicken with the cumin, garlic powder, sage, oregano, bay leaf powder, pepper, vinegar, and olive oil. Turn to coat. Refrigerate for at least 1 hour or overnight.

MEANWHILE, MAKE THE CABBAGE SLAW: In a large bowl, combine the cabbage, red onion, and lemon juice. Toss to coat.

MAKE THE SAUCE: In a medium bowl, whisk together the mayonnaise, ketchup, mustard, garlic powder, and 1 tablespoon water. Stir in the cilantro.

TO ASSEMBLE: Grease a grill or grill pan and heat over medium-high. Add the chicken and cook until the bottom is opaque and grill marks appear, 5 to 7 minutes. Flip and continue to cook until the second side is also opaque with grill marks and an instant-read thermometer registers 160°F, 5 to 7 minutes more. Transfer the chicken to a plate and cover with foil to keep warm.

Meanwhile, cut the plantains into thick matchsticks.

Pour 2 inches canola oil into a large, heavy-bottomed pot. Clip a thermometer to the side of the pot and heat the oil over medium-high heat to 350°F.

Carefully add the plantain slices and cook, turning occasionally, until golden brown and crisp, 3 to 5 minutes. Use a slotted spoon to transfer them to a plate lined with paper towels. Sprinkle with salt and let cool slightly.

Divide the chicken, plantains, and slaw among four plates. Serve with the sauce alongside.

Soy-Braised Chicken Drumsticks

Everyone knows the drumstick is the best part of the chicken—or at least the most fun to pick up and eat with your hands. When you put it in a sticky sweet sauce, that's when the party really starts. This brothy, gingery, super-garlicky sauce is everything, and this dish is a prime example of making a wildly flavorful meal out of ingredients that you probably have on hand already. We love to serve these drumsticks with rice to soak up every last drop. Satisfying. Easy. Delicious. It's the dinner trifecta.

SERVES 4

2 pounds chicken drumsticks

Kosher salt and freshly ground black pepper

2 tablespoons vegetable oil

10 garlic cloves

1½ cups chicken stock

¼ cup honey

¼ cup rice vinegar

¼ cup soy sauce

1 tablespoon grated fresh ginger

3 scallions, thinly sliced

1 tablespoon sesame seeds

2 teaspoons crushed red pepper flakes

Season the drumsticks with salt and black pepper. In a large Dutch oven, heat the oil over medium heat. Working in batches, add the drumsticks and cook, turning occasionally, until golden brown all over, 3 to 4 minutes per side. Transfer to a plate.

Add the garlic to the pot and cook, stirring occasionally, until golden brown, about 5 minutes. Use a slotted spoon to transfer the garlic to the plate with the chicken.

Drain the excess fat from the pot and return it to medium heat. Add the chicken stock and scrape up any browned bits from the bottom. Stir in the honey, vinegar, soy sauce, and ginger. Return the drumsticks and garlic to the pot along with any collected juices. Bring to a simmer and cook until an instant-read thermometer inserted in a drumstick registers 165°F, about 25 minutes.

Use tongs to transfer the drumsticks to a serving platter, keeping the sauce in the pot. Continue to cook over medium heat until the sauce has reduced by half and is thick enough to coat the back of a spoon, 8 to 10 minutes.

Spoon some of the sauce over the drumsticks. Top with the scallions, sesame seeds, and pepper flakes. Serve with the remaining sauce alongside.

Chorizo and Tomato Quiche

With a flaky, buttery crust and a wonderfully savory, decadent filling, this quiche is a surefire way to make dinner exciting. Spicy, fatty, and highly seasoned, Mexican chorizo is some of the most flavorful sausage around—you'll taste the vinegar and chile for sure. The tomatoes provide a welcome note of juicy sweetness, rounding out this perfect little quiche.

SERVES 8 TO 10

Flaky Pie Dough (page 59)

¼ pound fresh Mexican chorizo, casings removed

5 large eggs

1 cup whole milk

½ cup heavy cream

½ cup sliced scallions

1 tablespoon dried parsley

1 teaspoon garlic powder

½ teaspoon dried thyme

½ teaspoon kosher salt

¼ teaspoon freshly ground black pepper

1 cup grape tomatoes, halved

Preheat the oven to 350°F.

Line the pie shell with foil or parchment paper and fill it with pie weights, dried rice, or dried beans. Bake for 15 minutes. Lift out the foil to remove the pie weights. Return the crust to the oven and continue to bake until lightly golden brown, about 10 minutes more. Remove the crust, leaving the oven on.

Meanwhile, in a medium skillet, cook the chorizo over medium-high heat, breaking it up with a wooden spoon, until cooked through, 5 to 7 minutes. Use a slotted spoon to transfer the chorizo to a plate lined with paper towels.

In a large bowl, whisk together the eggs, milk, cream, scallions, parsley, garlic powder, thyme, salt, and pepper until smooth. Carefully pour the egg mixture into the pie crust. Sprinkle the chorizo and the tomatoes over the top.

Bake until the filling is set and no longer moves when you shake the pan, about 45 minutes. Let cool before slicing and serving.

Ras el Hanout Sheet-Pan Chicken

We are devotees of the sheet-pan meal, the perfect easy-to-prepare answer for many a weeknight dinner that serves a crowd in a snap and makes for fast clean up. Ras el hanout, a sweet, rich North African spice blend, is the star of the show in this chicken dish, infusing the meat and vegetables with a warm and comforting depth of flavor. Preserved Lemons (page 266) would be perfect on the side here. Steaming some rice while the sheet pan is in the oven, and tossing some green olives into it when it's done, wouldn't be a bad idea either.

SERVES 6 TO 8

1 head garlic, separated into cloves, plus 3 cloves

1 tablespoon grated fresh ginger

2½ tablespoons ras el hanout

1 teaspoon ground turmeric

2 tablespoons extra-virgin olive oil

Juice of 1 lemon

Kosher salt and freshly ground black pepper

3 pounds boneless, skinless chicken breasts

1 yellow onion, cut into wedges

1 medium butternut squash, peeled, seeded, and cut into 1-inch cubes

4 to 6 large carrots, chopped

½ cup chicken stock

Grate 3 of the garlic cloves into a large bowl. Add the ginger, ras el hanout, turmeric, 1 tablespoon of the olive oil, the lemon juice, ½ teaspoon salt, and ¼ teaspoon pepper and stir to form a paste. Add the chicken and massage the marinade into it. Marinate in the refrigerator for at least 4 hours or overnight. Remove from the refrigerator 30 minutes before cooking.

Preheat the oven to 425°F.

On a sheet pan, combine the onion, remaining whole garlic cloves, squash, and carrots with the remaining 1 tablespoon olive oil. Season with salt and pepper. Toss to combine, then spread the vegetables into a single layer. Pour ¼ cup of the chicken stock over the vegetables and roast for 20 minutes.

Remove the sheet pan from the oven and toss the vegetables. Add the chicken to the sheet pan, taking care not to crowd. Return to the oven and cook 10 minutes more. Remove again, pour the remaining ¼ cup chicken stock over the chicken and vegetables and flip the chicken breasts over. Return the sheet pan to the oven to roast until the chicken is opaque and an instant-read thermometer registers 165°F, 15 to 20 minutes more.

Serve immediately.

Pork Chops
with Seared Peaches

This is the perfect little late-summer number for two that's both eco-nomical and flavorful. Peaches, the season's greatest gift, are amazing with just about anything—and on their own—but they go especially well with pork chops. Look for firm ones to ensure they hold up to the heat. Serve this dish with Farro Salad (page 181) or Stone-Ground Grits with Scallions and Garlic-Chile Oil (page 182), and you've made an excellent pairing decision. Congrats!

SERVES 2

3 Thai chiles, thinly sliced

½ medium white onion, thinly sliced

4 garlic cloves, thinly sliced

¼ cup chopped fresh cilantro, plus leaves for serving

¼ cup soy sauce

¼ cup fish sauce

2 tablespoons honey

2 bone-in pork chops (about 8 ounces each)

2 tablespoons neutral oil

4 peaches, cut into ½-inch-thick slices

In a small bowl, combine the chiles, onion, garlic, cilantro, soy sauce, fish sauce, and honey. Place the pork chops in a resealable zip-top bag and pour in half of the marinade. Turn to coat. Refrigerate for at least 2 hours or overnight.

In a large cast-iron skillet, heat the oil over high heat. Add the pork chops and cook, undisturbed, until well browned on the bottom, about 5 minutes. Flip and continue to cook until well browned on the second side and an instant-read thermometer registers 145°F, 5 to 7 minutes more. Transfer to a cutting board and let rest.

Add the peaches to the same skillet over high heat. Sear until caramelized, about 3 minutes per side.

Serve the pork chops with the caramelized peaches and spoon the reserved marinade over the top. Garnish with fresh cilantro leaves and serve.

Curry-Butter Roast Chicken

May we present . . . a superlative way to cook a whole chicken that just happens to be an extremely low-hassle way, too? We are big fans of giving any chicken a big old butter massage preroast for a moisture-locking result and crispy skin every time. Here, we've amped it up with curry powder for a deep, complex flavor that we expect to become your new favorite thing. You're welcome.

SERVES 4 TO 6

4 tablespoons (½ stick) unsalted butter, at room temperature

2 garlic cloves, grated

1 tablespoon curry powder

Kosher salt and freshly ground black pepper

1 whole spatchcocked chicken (3½ to 4 pounds)

Preheat the oven to 325°F.

In a small bowl, combine the butter, garlic, and curry powder and use a fork to incorporate until smooth. Season generously with salt and pepper.

Pat the chicken dry and season with salt and pepper. Rub the butter all over the outside of the chicken, making sure it is completely covered. Use your fingers to gently loosen the skin from the meat and smear the butter underneath the skin.

Place the chicken on a sheet pan or in a large cast-iron skillet. Roast the chicken until an instant-read thermometer inserted into the breast registers 150°F and the thighs and legs register at least 165°F, about 1½ hours. (If the skin is beginning to burn before the chicken is done roasting, tent with a sheet of foil.)

Remove the chicken from the oven and let it rest for 10 minutes before carving and serving.

How to Spatchcock a Chicken

Discard the gizzards and neck from the chicken, then place it breast-side down on a cutting board. Using sharp kitchen shears and starting at the tail, cut along one side of the backbone up to the neck. Follow the same cut along the other side of the backbone and remove the backbone, discarding or saving it to use for stock. Turn the chicken breast-side up and firmly press down to break the breastbone and flatten the bird. Use the shears to remove the wing tips, discarding or reserving for stock.

Challah Chicken "Pot Pie"

A chicken pot pie as you probably know it has a rich, creamy filling (thanks to a butter-based sauce) under a light, flaky crust (butter doing its thing again). We absolutely love this dish, but we wanted a kosher version—meaning we had to find a way around mixing that delicious dairy with the meat. This super-satisfying take on the classic makes for a tasty alternative, and doubles as a perfect second act for stale bread and veggies languishing in the refrigerator. We used the traditional onion-celery-carrot trifecta, but feel free to get creative.

SERVES 6

1 tablespoon extra-virgin olive oil

½ pound boneless, skinless chicken thighs, cut into ½-inch cubes

¼ medium yellow onion, diced

3 celery stalks, sliced

2 medium carrots, sliced

2 teaspoons herbes de Provence

1 teaspoon garlic powder

1 teaspoon kosher salt, plus more to taste

2 cups chicken or vegetable stock

2 large eggs

¼ cup frozen peas

2 bay leaves

½ loaf day-old challah, torn into 2-inch cubes

Preheat the oven to 375°F.

In a Dutch oven, heat the olive oil over medium heat. Add the chicken, onion, celery, carrots, herbes de Provence, garlic powder, and salt. Cook, stirring occasionally, until the onions begin to soften, about 2 minutes. Cover and continue to cook until the onion and celery are translucent and the chicken is cooked through, about 5 minutes more.

Remove the lid and add the stock, scraping up any browned bits from the bottom of the pan. Increase the heat to high and bring to a boil, then turn off the heat. Taste and add more salt as needed.

Beat the eggs in a medium bowl. While whisking, add a ladleful of the hot liquid to the eggs. Add one more ladleful, continuing to whisk constantly. (Go slowly here; if you add too much hot liquid too quickly, you will end up with scrambled eggs.) Slowly pour the egg mixture back into the pot, whisking constantly, until incorporated.

Stir in the peas and bay leaves. Add the challah and push the pieces down to mostly (but not completely) submerge.

Cover, transfer to the oven, and bake until the challah has begun to absorb the liquid, about 15 minutes. Uncover and continue to bake until the dish has firmed into a soft bread pudding consistency and the challah is lightly toasted, about 15 minutes more.

To serve, discard the bay leaves and scoop the pudding into bowls.

Sticky Lemongrass Pork and Herb Salad

File this one under Beautiful Studies in Contrasts: sweet, acidic pork meets crisp, refreshing herbs and crunchy veggies. It's an ultimate warm-weather dinner salad that's all about the play of sweet, sour, bitter, salty, and a healthy dose of umami (don't sleep on the fish sauce, in either the marinade or the vinaigrette). We love using rice noodles as a base to bring the dish even deeper into main-course territory, but you can easily keep this just a pork and salad affair.

SERVES 2 TO 4

For the pork

½ cup packed light brown sugar

¼ cup granulated sugar

⅓ cup fish sauce

1 stalk lemongrass, roughly chopped

6 garlic cloves, chopped

1 small yellow onion, roughly chopped

1 Thai chile, roughly chopped

3 tablespoons vegetable oil

1 teaspoon freshly ground black pepper

2½ pounds pork loin

For the salad

1 teaspoon honey

2 tablespoons fish sauce

Juice of 1 lime

1 tablespoon distilled white vinegar

Kosher salt

1 small head lettuce, shredded

½ cup shredded napa cabbage

1 large carrot, cut into matchsticks

1 English cucumber, cut into matchsticks

For serving

¼ cup chopped fresh basil

¼ cup chopped fresh mint

1 small bunch cilantro, roughly chopped

Cooked rice noodles (optional)

3 scallions, thinly sliced

Lime wedges

MAKE THE PORK: In a medium bowl, combine the brown sugar, granulated sugar, fish sauce, lemongrass, garlic, onion, chile, oil, and pepper and whisk to dissolve the sugars. Add the pork and turn to coat. Marinate in the refrigerator for at least 2 hours or overnight. About 45 minutes before cooking, remove the pork from the fridge.

Prepare a grill for two-zone cooking: medium-high heat on one side, with a cooler section off to the side. (Alternatively, heat a grill pan or cast-iron skillet over medium-high heat.)

Add the pork to the hot side of the grill (or grill pan) and cook until beginning to char, 2 to 3 minutes per side. Move the meat to the cooler area of the grill (or reduce the heat under the pan to medium-low) and continue to cook until an instant-read thermometer inserted into the thickest part of the pork registers 145°F, about 10 minutes more. Transfer the pork to a cutting board to rest.

MAKE THE SALAD: In a large bowl, whisk together the honey, fish sauce, lime juice, vinegar, and a pinch of salt. Add the lettuce, cabbage, carrot, and cucumber to the vinaigrette and toss to coat.

TO SERVE: In a small bowl, toss together the basil, mint, and ¼ cup of the cilantro.

Thinly slice the pork. Divide the noodles (if using) among plates and top with the salad, herb mixture, sliced pork, and scallions. Sprinkle with the remaining cilantro and serve with lime wedges alongside for squeezing.

Beef
and Lamb

Korean Beef Bulgogi

Bulgogi, which literally means "fire-meat," is deeply marinated, thinly sliced cuts of beef, charred over fiery coals. Mouthwatering, right? Originally a delicacy of North Korea, bulgogi is now one of the most popular dishes throughout both Koreas, found everywhere from specialty barbecue restaurants to fast-food burger joints. This recipe adapts all the flavors of bulgogi into a stir-fry loaded with veggies. It's a sure-fire crowd-pleaser thanks to a knock-out marinade that shows off our ideal balance of the spice-salt-sugar trifecta that results in tender meat every time. If you can't find Korean peppers, milder bell peppers will work, too.

SERVES 4 TO 6

For the beef

¼ medium white onion, roughly chopped

3 garlic cloves, chopped

½ scallion, thinly sliced

3 tablespoons soy sauce

3 tablespoons mirin

2 tablespoons sugar

1 tablespoon sesame oil

1 tablespoon sesame seeds

1 teaspoon freshly ground black pepper

1 pound beef tenderloin, top sirloin, or skirt steak, cut into bite-size pieces

For the stir-fry

2 tablespoons vegetable oil

2 ounces shiitake mushrooms, thinly sliced

1 medium white onion, thinly sliced

½ carrot, halved lengthwise and sliced into half-moons

1 scallion, sliced on the diagonal

1 Korean red pepper, seeded and sliced on the diagonal

2 Korean green peppers, seeded and sliced on the diagonal

Kosher salt

For serving

Sesame seeds

Sesame oil

Steamed rice

Lettuce leaves

MARINATE THE BEEF: In a food processor, combine the onion, garlic, scallion, soy sauce, mirin, sugar, sesame oil, sesame seeds, and black pepper and pulse until smooth. Transfer the marinade to a large bowl or resealable zip-top bag. Add the beef, turn to coat, and marinate at room temperature for at least 30 minutes or overnight.

MAKE THE STIR-FRY: In a large skillet, heat the vegetable oil over high heat. Remove the beef from the marinade, allowing any excess to drip off, and add to the skillet. Cook, undisturbed, until the meat has begun to char slightly on the bottom, 2 to 3 minutes. Add the mushrooms and cook, stirring occasionally, until slightly softened, about 5 minutes. Add the onion and carrot and cook, stirring, until the onion is translucent and the carrot is slightly softened, about 5 minutes. Add the scallion, red pepper, and green peppers and season with salt. Cook, stirring, until the peppers are beginning to soften, about 2 minutes. Remove the skillet from the heat.

Garnish with sesame seeds and sesame oil to taste and serve family-style with rice and/or lettuce leaves alongside.

NOTE: If you freeze your meat for 30 or so minutes, slicing it up will be a cinch. (Works great on chicken, too!)

Brisket

Brisket is one of those classic dishes to have in your repertoire. Don't worry; we've got you. The braise here—based in bourbon, with ketchup and soy sauce providing a flavorful punch—is incredibly easy, and the stunning results will earn you praise for your culinary prowess. We like to use a "first-cut" brisket, as it's leaner and has an even thickness, though you can also use a second-cut, or even double or triple the recipe to use a full brisket. Other than the meat, you don't need to splurge on anything here—whether you're using brandy, bourbon, or wine, no need to use up anything you'd rather drink. Change it up with flavored ketchup (we like Heinz's balsamic or sriracha) for interesting combinations. For best results, start the brisket the day before you intend to serve it so it can rest overnight in the fridge. Pair this with potatoes, egg noodles, or our favorite, potato kugel—all champions at soaking up the delicious broth!

SERVES 4 TO 6

1 first-cut brisket
(2 to 3 pounds)

Kosher salt and freshly ground black pepper

4 tablespoons neutral oil, plus more as needed

2 large yellow onions, thinly sliced

2 large Vidalia or red onions, thinly sliced

2 large white onions, thinly sliced

5 garlic cloves, pressed or minced

2 tablespoons tomato paste

½ cup bourbon or brandy, or ¼ cup red wine

¼ cup apple cider vinegar

¾ cup packed dark brown sugar

1 cup ketchup

2 tablespoons soy sauce

1 cup beef, chicken, or vegetable stock

1 or 2 tablespoons cornstarch or potato starch (optional)

Pat the brisket dry. Set the brisket on a wire rack over a layer of paper towels and season it generously with salt. Let sit at room temperature for about 1 hour. Pat the brisket dry again (the salt will have drawn out more moisture) and season with pepper, pressing it into the meat.

Preheat the oven to 250°F.

CONTINUED

Meanwhile, in a Dutch oven, heat 2 tablespoons of the oil over medium-low heat. Add all the onions, season with salt, and cook, stirring occasionally, until translucent and golden, 8 to 10 minutes. Using a slotted spoon, transfer the onions to a bowl.

Add the remaining 2 tablespoons oil to the Dutch oven and increase the heat to high. Add the brisket and cook, undisturbed, until golden brown on the bottom, about 4 minutes. Flip the brisket over and continue to cook until golden brown on the second side, about 4 minutes more. (If your brisket has flat edges, sear those as well.) Transfer the brisket back to the wire rack, this time over a layer of foil, to rest.

Reduce the heat under the Dutch oven to medium-low. Add the garlic and tomato paste and cook, stirring constantly, until the garlic is golden brown and the tomato paste is brick-red and slightly caramelized, 2 to 3 minutes. Gradually add the bourbon, scraping up any browned bits from the pot. If the liquid evaporates, add a splash more so the bottom is barely covered.

Add the vinegar, again scrape up any browned bits, and bring the mixture to a boil. Add the brown sugar and stir to dissolve. Stir in the ketchup and soy sauce, then add the stock.

Return the onions and any collected juices to the pot and bring the mixture to a simmer. Carefully return the brisket to the pot, nestling it under the onions and using a large spoon to cover any exposed meat.

Cover the pot and transfer it to the oven. Roast for 40 minutes, then remove the pot from the oven and flip the brisket, again making sure to submerge the meat under the onions and broth. Cover and return the pot to the oven. Repeat this process every 40 minutes until the meat is fork-tender, at least 3 hours or up to 4 hours depending on the size and cut of meat.

Transfer the brisket to a roasting pan, sheet pan, or serving platter, leaving the onions and broth in the pot. Tent the brisket with foil and let rest at room temperature for at least 1 hour and up to 2 hours, or refrigerate overnight.

If the broth seems thin, return it to the stove over low heat. Transfer a ladleful of broth to a small bowl and whisk in 1 tablespoon of the cornstarch. Pour the mixture back into the broth and cook, stirring, until thickened, about 2 minutes. Repeat with an additional ladleful and another tablespoon of cornstarch if needed. (If refrigerating the brisket overnight, store the broth covered in the refrigerator until ready to serve.)

Transfer the brisket to a cutting board and slice against the grain. Return the brisket to the broth to warm through, 2 to 3 minutes. Serve family-style.

Adjusting the Seasoning of Your Brisket

It's nerve-wracking to prepare a large piece of meat that is meant to simmer for long periods of time! We recommend tasting the broth with each flip of the brisket. If, along the way, you're worried about the flavor, here are a few recommendations for course correcting.

- If it's not salty enough, add more soy sauce.

- If it tastes shallow, flat, or a little bland, add some garlic powder or smoked paprika.

- If it tastes deeply rich, but needs a touch of brightness, add a dash of vinegar.

- If after all the sugar, bourbon, and ketchup it's still not sweet enough . . . you should probably go see a doctor.

Rib Eye Steak with Anchovy Butter and Homemade French Fries

This one's for all the 'chovy lovers out there—and it's even for the 'chovy-wary. We're not gonna say anchovy "haters," because you shouldn't knock 'em till you try this recipe. They are the hero of this decadent steak dinner, adding a depth of brininess that accompanies every bite. (And if you want to go all-in on the anchovy adventure, you could serve this steak with the Any-Greens Caesar Salad on page 31.) Life is about reconsidering your assumptions and embracing the unknown, so start here.

SERVES 4 TO 6

1 (2-pound) rib eye steak

Kosher salt and freshly ground black pepper

3 Yukon Gold potatoes (about 2 pounds), scrubbed and cut into matchsticks

6 tablespoons extra-virgin olive oil

Anchovy Butter (recipe follows) or salted butter, for serving

Season the steak all over with salt and pepper. Set on a wire rack fitted into a sheet pan and refrigerate, uncovered, for at least 2 hours or overnight.

Preheat the oven to 450°F. Line a baking sheet with parchment paper.

Bring a large pot of salted water to a boil. Add the potatoes and cook until slightly softened, 7 to 8 minutes. Drain, return the potatoes to the pot, and let cool slightly. Drizzle with 3 tablespoons of the olive oil and toss gently to coat. Season with salt and pepper. Spread the potatoes out on the prepared baking sheet in a single layer and bake, tossing the potatoes occasionally, until golden and crispy, 40 to 50 minutes.

Heat a large cast-iron skillet over medium-high heat. Add the remaining 3 tablespoons olive oil to the skillet. Add the steak and cook, flipping every 2 to 3 minutes, until a dark crust forms and an instant-read thermometer registers 125°F for medium-rare, 12 to 15 minutes total. Transfer the steak to a cutting board, top with anchovy butter, and let rest.

Cut the steak into slices and divide among plates. Add fries to each plate. Serve with more anchovy butter alongside as desired.

CONTINUED

Anchovy Butter

MAKES ½ CUP

8 tablespoons (1 stick) unsalted butter, at room temperature

6 oil-packed anchovies, drained and finely chopped

2 garlic cloves, grated

¼ cup chopped fresh parsley

2 teaspoons Aleppo pepper or crushed red pepper flakes

Kosher salt and freshly ground black pepper

In a small bowl, combine the butter, anchovies, garlic, parsley, Aleppo pepper, salt, and black pepper to taste and mash with a fork to combine. Lay out a piece of parchment or plastic wrap on the counter and transfer the butter mixture onto it. Roll the butter into a small log. Transfer to the refrigerator to chill until firm, at least 1 hour. Store refrigerated for up to 4 weeks or frozen for up to 3 months.

Ground Beef with Sofrito, Capers, and Olives

Inspired by Puerto Rican picadillo, this hearty beef dish is brightened up by green peppers and a blend of herbs—pair it with any vegetable under the sun for a singular and satisfying meal. The name picadillo comes from the Spanish verb picar, *"to mince," and it's a popular dish throughout Latin America and the Philippines, with lots of regional variations and applications. At its core, it's a simple stir-fry, but packed with flavor from the briny capers and olives. And let's not forget the delicious sofrito base of onion, bell peppers, and garlic that features sazón seasoning, which is a powerhouse punch of savory, complex taste. You'll have extra sofrito after making this—save it and use it later to spoon over grilled meat, whisk into an omelet, or start a pot of hearty soup.*

SERVES 3 TO 4

2 tablespoons extra-virgin olive oil

¼ cup Sofrito (recipe follows)

1 teaspoon capers, chopped

1 tablespoon chopped pitted Spanish olives

1 pound ground beef

3 tablespoons tomato paste

Fresh cilantro, for serving

Steamed rice, for serving

In a large skillet, heat the olive oil over medium heat. Add the sofrito and cook, stirring occasionally, until golden and fragrant, 2 to 3 minutes. Add the capers and olives and cook, stirring, until softened, about 3 minutes more.

Add the ground beef and cook, breaking it up with a wooden spoon, until browned and cooked through, 3 to 5 minutes more. Stir in the tomato paste and 1 cup water and cook, stirring, until the tomato paste is incorporated and the liquid has evaporated, 8 to 10 minutes.

To serve, divide the ground beef among plates and top with fresh cilantro alongside rice.

Beef and Lamb

CONTINUED

Sofrito

MAKES ABOUT 2 CUPS

1 medium yellow onion, chopped

1 green bell pepper, chopped

1 red bell pepper, chopped

10 garlic cloves, peeled

2 scallions, chopped

½ bunch cilantro

3 tablespoons sazón (see Note, page 101)

1 tablespoon extra-virgin olive oil

In a food processor, combine the onion, green bell pepper, red bell pepper, garlic, scallions, cilantro, sazón, and olive oil. Pulse until the mixture is well combined but still chunky. Store refrigerated in an airtight container for up to 1 week or freeze in ice-cube trays and store for up to 6 months.

Simple Smash Burgers

Smash burger is the only *way we burger. It is exactly what it sounds like:*
You flatten down the patties while they're cooking so they come out thin
and crispy, but still perfectly juicy. One of the keys to achieving this is to
start with a loosely formed 4-ounce ball made with ground beef that's at
least 20% fat. Pop it on a potato bun, dress it up with all the toppings, and
we promise—you'll never look back.

MAKES 4 BURGERS

1 tablespoon kosher salt

1 teaspoon freshly ground
black pepper

1 teaspoon onion powder

1 teaspoon garlic powder

1 pound ground beef (80/20)

1 tablespoon neutral oil

4 potato buns, split and
toasted

Optional toppings

Pepper Jack cheese

Caramelized onions

Sliced tomatoes

Arugula

Thousand Island dressing

In a large bowl, combine the salt, pepper, onion powder, and garlic powder. Add the ground beef and using your hands, gently incorporate the spice mixture into the meat, making sure not to overmix. Set aside for 15 minutes to let the meat absorb the seasoning.

Divide the beef mixture into 4 equal portions and form each into a loose ball.

Heat a large cast-iron skillet over high heat. Add the oil and place one ball in the center of the pan. Using another cast-iron skillet, metal spatula, or trowel, immediately smash down on the patty to flatten it. Cook until browned on the bottom, 1 to 2 minutes. Flip the patty and continue to cook on the second side, 1 to 2 minutes more. Transfer the finished burger to a plate and tent with foil to keep warm. Repeat with the remaining patties.

To serve, divide the burgers among the potato buns and add desired toppings.

Salt-Crusted Steak and Onions

What's all this about a salt crust, you ask? To put it simply, salt acts as a moisture seal to lock in all those delectable meaty juices so that you get the pleasure of a perfectly juicy steak. Show this to your dinner guest before you plate it—they'll be very impressed by your technique. Add a simple green vegetable alongside for a well-rounded meal.

SERVES 2

1 pound New York strip or rib eye steak

Freshly ground black pepper

3 cups kosher salt, plus more as needed

¼ cup extra-virgin olive oil

1½ tablespoons smoked paprika

1 large yellow onion, halved

Remove the steak from the refrigerator 1 hour before cooking. Season both sides with pepper.

Preheat the oven to 350°F. Line a sheet pan with parchment paper.

In a medium bowl, combine the salt, ⅔ cup water, the olive oil, and paprika. Stir to mix well; it should resemble sandcastle-quality damp sand—wet enough to cover the steak without falling apart, but not so wet that it would slide off. Add more salt or water as needed.

Pour half of the salt mixture onto the lined sheet pan and using your hands, smooth it into an even layer. On one side of the baking sheet, nestle the onion halves cut side-down into the salt mixture.

Transfer to the oven and roast for 20 minutes.

Remove the baking sheet from the oven and add the steak to the open side, nestling it into in the salt mixture. Pile the remaining salt mixture over the steak and onion, covering completely and pressing to adhere. Return the pan to the oven and continue to roast until an instant-read thermometer registers 130°F to 135°F for medium-rare, 15 to 20 minutes more.

Let the steak rest for 5 minutes. Use a wooden spoon to crack through the crust. Transfer the steak and onion to a cutting board and brush off any excess salt. Cut the steak against the grain and arrange on a serving platter. Thinly slice the onion and add to the platter. Serve.

Albondigas Soup

Albóndiga means "meatball" in Spanish. But in Mexican cuisine, the word is often shorthand for a rich and savory soup—typically served at celebrations like birthdays or baptisms—studded with vegetables and loaded with, yes, meatballs. And about those meatballs... they're flecked with mint, an herb not often associated with chicken or pork. But it more than earns a place of pride with a welcome cooling quality. And instead of bread crumbs, binder duty falls to cooked white rice, giving a starchy hold without a dense ball. A hearty pot of albondigas is a perfect excuse to make any day special.

SERVES 4 TO 6

For the soup

2 tablespoons extra-virgin olive oil

½ medium white onion, minced

2 garlic cloves, minced

1 celery stalk, cut into 1-inch pieces

1 medium carrot, cut into 1-inch pieces

1 medium russet potato, cut into 1-inch pieces

1 teaspoon ground cumin

1 teaspoon dried oregano

2 teaspoons kosher salt

1 (14.5-ounce) can diced tomatoes

4 cups chicken broth or stock

For the meatballs

½ pound ground pork

½ pound ground chicken

½ medium white onion, minced

2 garlic cloves, minced

2 tablespoons chopped fresh mint

2 tablespoons chopped fresh marjoram

2 tablespoons dried oregano

2 teaspoons kosher salt

1 large egg

½ cup cooked white rice

2 tablespoons extra-virgin olive oil, plus more as needed

Cilantro leaves, for serving

MAKE THE SOUP: In a Dutch oven, heat the olive oil over medium heat. Add the onion and cook, stirring occasionally, until soft and translucent, about 4 minutes. Add the garlic, celery, carrot, potato, cumin, oregano, and salt. Continue to cook, stirring occasionally, until the garlic and cumin are fragrant and the vegetables are starting to release liquid, about 2 minutes.

Add the tomatoes and broth. Increase the heat to high and bring to a boil, then cover and reduce the heat to low. Simmer until the potatoes and carrots are tender, about 10 minutes.

CONTINUED

MEANWHILE, MAKE THE MEATBALLS: In a large bowl, combine the pork, chicken, onion, garlic, mint, marjoram, oregano, salt, egg, and rice. Using your hands, gently mix until well incorporated. Roll the mixture into 1-inch balls; you should have about 20.

In a medium skillet, heat the olive oil over medium-high heat. Working in batches, add the meatballs and cook, turning, until browned on the outside and cooked through, 3 to 5 minutes per side. Transfer to a plate. Repeat with the remaining meatballs, adding more oil to the pan as needed between batches.

Add the meatballs and any collected juices to the soup. Simmer over medium-low heat until the meatballs are warmed through, about 5 minutes.

Ladle the soup and meatballs into bowls. Finish with cilantro before serving.

Lamb Meatballs with Yogurt Sauce

In this recipe, a delicious warming spice blend infuses meatballs that are cooked with rice to help hold them together. These rich flavor bombs sit in a super-tasty sauce, and a dollop of zingy yogurt both offsets and ties together these elements. Trust us—you will want to use this yogurt sauce on everything from grilled meat to roasted veggies. It refreshes your palate with every bite.

SERVES 6 TO 8

For the red onion yogurt

2 to 3 tablespoons minced red onion

¼ teaspoon kosher salt

½ teaspoon cumin seeds or coriander seeds

⅓ cup plain whole-milk Greek yogurt

For the meatballs

1 pound ground lamb

1 teaspoon kosher salt

1 teaspoon freshly ground black pepper

2 tablespoons very finely minced fresh mint or oregano

3 tablespoons plain whole-milk Greek yogurt

⅓ cup cold cooked rice

For the braising sauce

3 tablespoons neutral oil

3 garlic cloves, chopped

1½ cups chopped red onion (about 1 medium onion)

1 jalapeño or fresno pepper, minced (optional)

1 medium tomato, chopped

1 teaspoon kosher salt

Mint, for serving

Parsley, for serving

MAKE THE RED ONION YOGURT: In a small bowl, toss the onion with the salt. Heat a small skillet over low heat and add the cumin seeds. Cook, stirring constantly, until the cumin is fragrant, about 20 seconds. Remove the skillet from the heat. Add the yogurt to the red onion mixture and stir in the toasted seeds. Refrigerate until serving time.

MAKE THE MEATBALLS: In a medium bowl, combine the lamb, salt, pepper, and mint and use your hands to gently mix. Add the yogurt and rice and gently fold to incorporate. Set a small bowl of water near your work station. Divide the meat mixture into 4 equal portions. Dip one hand into the bowl of water and use it to form each portion into 6 meatballs.

CONTINUED

MAKE THE BRAISING SAUCE: In a large skillet, heat the oil over medium-high heat. Add the garlic, red onion, and jalapeño (if using). Cook, stirring occasionally, until the onion is translucent and beginning to brown, 5 to 8 minutes. Reduce the heat to medium and add the tomato and salt. Continue to cook, stirring, until the tomato is breaking down, about 3 minutes more. Add 1 cup water and bring to a simmer.

Working in batches, carefully add the meatballs in a single layer. Reduce the heat to medium-low, cover, and cook for about 10 minutes, checking occasionally for even cooking and rotating the pot or meatballs if needed. Uncover and continue to cook until the sauce has reduced slightly and is thickened, about 10 minutes more.

To serve, divide among bowls, serve with the red onion yogurt alongside, and garnish with mint and parsley.

Bolognese

The sum is definitely more than the parts in this incredibly rich Bolognese. You don't need anything fussy—just humble ingredients and time to develop delicious depth of flavor. You can use ground lamb or beef; lamb lends a rich earthiness to the dish, while the beef version is a comforting classic. And the chef's kiss at the end? Finish the sauce with a pat of butter and plenty of Parmesan and fresh cracked pepper. It's the kind of culinary magic that, until now, you thought could only be imparted by an Italian grandma.

SERVES 6

2 tablespoons extra-virgin olive oil

2 tablespoons unsalted butter, plus more (optional) for serving

¾ cup chopped yellow onion

⅔ cup chopped celery

⅔ cup chopped carrot

1 pound ground lamb or beef

1 teaspoon kosher salt

Freshly ground black pepper

1 cup whole milk

4 sprigs fresh thyme

1 bay leaf

1½ cups dry white wine, such as Sauvignon Blanc or Pinot Grigio

1 (28-ounce) can crushed tomatoes

Cooked pasta or roasted veggies of your choice, for serving

Parmesan cheese, for serving

In a large saucepan, heat the olive oil and butter together over medium heat. When the butter is melted, add the onion and cook, stirring occasionally, until soft and translucent but not yet browned, 6 to 8 minutes. Add the celery and carrot and cook, stirring occasionally, until slightly softened, about 4 minutes.

Add the ground meat, salt, and pepper to taste. Cook, breaking up the meat with a wooden spoon, until browned and cooked through, 8 to 10 minutes. Add the milk and cook, stirring often, until the mixture is thickened and fully reduced, about 8 minutes more. Add the thyme, bay leaf, and wine. Reduce the heat to medium-low and cook, stirring occasionally, until most of the liquid has evaporated, 30 to 40 minutes.

Stir in the tomatoes and their juices. Reduce the heat to low and cook, stirring occasionally, for at least 45 minutes and up to 3 hours; the longer you cook the sauce, the more the flavors will meld, mellow, and deepen. Discard the thyme stems and bay leaves.

To serve, toss the Bolognese with pasta or roasted veggies. Top with a pat of butter, if desired, and plenty of fresh Parmesan and black pepper.

NOTE: If you happen to have a Parmesan cheese rind in your fridge or freezer, add it to the sauce along with the wine for even more richness and depth of flavor. It's absolutely not necessary but a great addition if you have it! This trick works well in soups and stews, too.

Pasta
and Grains

Fresh Tagliatelle with Mint Pesto and Shrimp

Welcome to handmade pasta land, a magical place where noodles are melt-in-your-mouth good and anything you put on them will be amazing. Once you've made this pasta dough (flour, eggs, and salt—that's it!), you can turn it into whatever shape your heart desires. Here, we keep it simple by cutting the pasta into the shape known as tagliatelle, a long, flat noodle, which we then toss in a mint-and-basil pesto and top with shrimp for a complete and filling meal.

SERVES 4 TO 6

Fresh Tagliatelle (recipe follows) or store-bought

Kosher salt

½ cup pine nuts, toasted

2 garlic cloves, roughly chopped

2 serrano chiles, seeded and roughly chopped

4 cups fresh mint leaves

1 cup fresh basil leaves

¼ cup fresh lemon juice

1 cup extra-virgin olive oil

Freshly ground black pepper

½ pound medium shrimp, peeled and deveined

Red pepper flakes (optional)

Bring a large pot of salted water to a boil. Add the tagliatelle and cook until tender, about 2 minutes. Reserving ½ cup pasta cooking water, drain the pasta.

Meanwhile, in a food processor, pulse together the pine nuts, garlic, and chiles until combined. Add the mint, basil, and lemon juice and pulse until smooth, stopping to scrape down the sides of the bowl as needed. With the motor running, slowly stream in ¾ cup of the olive oil and continue to pulse until the oil is incorporated. Taste the pesto and add salt and pepper as needed.

In a large skillet, heat the remaining ¼ cup olive oil over medium-high heat. Add the shrimp, season with 1 teaspoon salt and pepper to taste and cook until the shrimp are pink and opaque, about 2 minutes per side.

Add the pesto and tagliatelle to the shrimp. Add the reserved pasta cooking water, 1 tablespoon at a time, and toss until the pasta is well coated and glossy. Taste and add more seasoning as desired.

Divide the pasta among plates and serve with crushed red pepper flakes, if using.

CONTINUED

Fresh Tagliatelle

SERVES 4 TO 6

5 ounces semolina flour

5 ounces all-purpose flour

1½ teaspoons kosher salt

2 large eggs

2 large egg yolks

Pour the flours and salt into the bowl of a stand mixer fitted with the paddle. With the mixer running on low, add the whole eggs, one at a time, then add the egg yolks, until the dough comes together.

Switch to the dough hook and knead until smooth and silky, 8 to 10 minutes. Turn out the dough and shape it into a round. Wrap the round tightly in plastic wrap and refrigerate for at least 45 minutes or overnight.

Line a baking sheet with parchment paper. Divide the pasta dough into 4 equal portions. In a stand mixer fitted with the pasta attachment, a pasta machine, or with a rolling pin, roll each portion into a ¹⁄₁₆-inch-thick rectangle. Flour the pasta sheets. Starting at a short side, roll them up into cylinders and cut crosswise into ½-inch-wide pieces. Separate the strands, dust with flour again, and lay out on the lined baking sheet to dry for 20 minutes before cooking.

Potato Gnocchi with Brown Butter and Sage

Gnocchi are their absolutely most delicious if you boil them first, and then pan-fry. This pillowy potato pasta becomes crispy and golden on the out-side (yes, please), as well as perfectly cloaked in sauce (and thank you). Here, that sauce is a classic accompaniment of brown butter infused with soft, woodsy sage. If you haven't tried making your own gnocchi yet, this is your chance. It's quite easy, and you'll feel extra proud of having whipped up this beauty completely from scratch.

SERVES 2 TO 4

1½ pounds russet potatoes, scrubbed

1 cup all-purpose flour, plus more for dusting

Kosher salt

2 large egg yolks

8 tablespoons (1 stick) unsalted butter, cut into cubes

4 to 6 fresh sage leaves

Freshly ground black pepper

2 ounces Parmesan cheese, grated

Preheat the oven to 400°F.

Pierce the potatoes all over with a fork. Bake until very tender, about 1 hour. Remove and let cool.

When the potatoes are cool enough to handle, halve them length-wise and scoop out the flesh, discarding the skins. Press the potato flesh through a ricer or food mill into a large bowl (or mash well). Add the flour and 1½ teaspoons salt and stir to combine. Stir in the egg yolks and mix until a dough comes together.

Line a baking sheet with parchment paper and dust the parch-ment with flour. On a lightly floured surface, turn out the dough and divide it in half. Using your hands, shape each half into a long rope about ¾ inch thick. Slice the ropes crosswise into ¾-inch-long pieces. If desired, roll each piece over the tines of a fork to create ridges. Place the gnocchi on the prepared baking sheet. Let dry for about 20 minutes.

CONTINUED

Pasta and Grains

Bring a large pot of salted water to a boil. Add half of the gnocchi and cook until they rise to the surface, about 4 minutes. Using a slotted spoon, transfer the gnocchi to a plate. Repeat with the remaining gnocchi.

Heat a large skillet over medium-low heat. Add the butter and cook, tilting the pan constantly to move the butter around, until melted. Continue to cook as the butter foams and starts to brown, swirling the pan occasionally, 3 to 4 minutes more. Add the sage and cook until fragrant and crispy, about 1 minute.

Add the boiled gnocchi to the butter sauce and stir gently to coat and warm through, 1 to 2 minutes. Season with salt and pepper, then divide among bowls. Top with the grated Parmesan and serve.

Hawaii-Style Macaroni Salad

If you've ever had a Hawaii-style plate-lunch, you know that there's one thing that accompanies every dish . . . a creamy, tangy mac salad. It works wonders alongside sweet grilled meats, including the classics like SPAM musubi and smoky kālua *pig, complementing the flavors and textures perfectly. Even if you're not on an island in the middle of the Pacific, you'll love this take on the pasta side dish.* Tōgarashi *is a zippy, zesty Japanese chili blend; if you can't find it, you can substitute chili powder here. And to get max Hawaii, add some pineapple right before you serve.*

SERVES 6 TO 8

1 tablespoon plus 1 teaspoon kosher salt

1 pound elbow macaroni

¼ cup grated white onion

2 tablespoons apple cider vinegar

¼ teaspoon garlic powder

2 cups mayonnaise

½ cup whole milk

1 tablespoon sugar

1 teaspoon tōgarashi

½ teaspoon freshly ground black pepper

¼ cup sliced scallions

¼ cup shredded carrot

¼ cup diced celery

Chopped fresh pineapple (optional)

Bring a large pot of water to a boil. Add 1 tablespoon of the salt and pour in the macaroni. Cook to al dente according to the package directions. Drain.

In a large bowl, combine the onion, vinegar, and garlic powder. Add the cooked macaroni and toss to combine. Let sit for about 10 minutes.

Meanwhile, in a serving bowl, whisk together the mayonnaise, milk, sugar, tōgarashi, the remaining 1 teaspoon salt, and the pepper until smooth. Add the macaroni mixture and toss to coat in the dressing. Add the scallions, carrot, and celery and toss to combine. Cover and refrigerate for at least 2 hours before serving. If desired, stir in some pineapple.

Late-Night Anchovy Spaghetti

If hunger strikes when the stores are dark, the restaurants are closed, and the delivery windows don't open until morning, you'll have to find something in your pantry. And we're willing to bet you have the makings of this savory, salty pasta dish already there. Bursting with flavor, this dish is one to be enjoyed in the dark or with someone you like very, very much. This recipe might just be the epitome of what we mean when we say Make This Tonight. . . .

SERVES 4

Kosher salt

1 pound spaghetti or other long pasta

2 tablespoons unsalted butter or extra-virgin olive oil

1 (2-ounce) tin oil-packed anchovy, drained (10 to 12 fillets)

4 garlic cloves, pressed or thinly sliced

Pinch of crushed red pepper flakes

½ cup dry white wine, such as Pinot Grigio or Sauvignon Blanc

Pitted Kalamata or other black olives, sliced

Freshly grated Parmesan cheese, for serving

Fresh parsley, for serving

Bring a large pot of salted water to a boil. Add the spaghetti and cook until slightly softened, 4 to 5 minutes. Turn off the heat and let the spaghetti continue to cook in the water until al dente, 4 to 5 minutes more. Drain.

Meanwhile, in a large skillet, melt the butter over medium-high heat. Add the anchovies and cook, breaking them down a bit with a wooden spoon, about 2 minutes. Add the garlic and pepper flakes and stir into the anchovies until fragrant, about 1 minute more.

Add the wine and continue to cook, stirring, until the anchovies melt into a paste and the wine is reduced by half, 1 to 2 minutes more. Add the drained spaghetti to the skillet and toss to coat evenly. Stir in the olives and remove the skillet from the heat.

Divide the pasta among bowls and sprinkle with the Parmesan and parsley. Serve.

Sheet-Pan Gnocchi Primavera

Bursting with vegetables, cheese, and crisped gnocchi, this sheet-pan party will liven up any weeknight, and the bonus is that the leftovers hold up really well. This recipe is your permission to go to the farmers' market, pick out the most beautiful produce with reckless abandon, and throw it all together. Though broccoli and cauliflower are featured in our version, you can change up the vegetables to keep it interesting throughout the seasons—swap in chopped hearty greens or green beans and asparagus, a trio of bell peppers for a colorful burst, or squash, zucchini, and fresh beans. You can use the homemade gnocchi recipe on page 163 (skip the sauce) or any store-bought potato gnocchi.

SERVES 4 TO 6

2 cups broccoli florets

1 cup cauliflower florets

2 cups cherry tomatoes

4 shallots, thinly sliced

8 garlic cloves, minced

3 tablespoons extra-virgin olive oil

Kosher salt and freshly ground black pepper

1 pound potato gnocchi, homemade (page 163) or store-bought

4 ounces crumbled feta cheese

For the pesto

⅓ cup walnuts, toasted

2 cups packed fresh basil leaves

½ teaspoon flaky salt, plus more to taste

¼ teaspoon freshly ground black pepper, plus more to taste

¼ cup extra-virgin olive oil

For serving

Lemon wedges

Freshly shaved Parmesan cheese

Flaky salt

Preheat the oven to 425°F.

On a sheet pan, combine the broccoli, cauliflower, tomatoes, shallots, and garlic. Drizzle with the olive oil, season with kosher salt and pepper, and toss to combine. Roast for 10 minutes.

Remove the pan from the oven. Add the gnocchi and feta and toss to combine. Return to the oven and roast until the gnocchi are cooked through, about 15 minutes more. Remove from the oven and transfer to a large bowl.

MEANWHILE, MAKE THE PESTO: In a food processor, combine the walnuts, basil, flaky salt, and pepper. Pulse for about 30 seconds until the walnuts are roughly chopped. Add the olive oil and pulse a few more times until mixed well. Taste and add seasoning as needed. Add the pesto to the bowl with the gnocchi and gently toss to coat.

Divide the pasta among bowls. Serve immediately with lemon wedges, Parmesan, and flaky salt.

Grandma's Lasagna

Lasagna is the ultimate comfort food—there's just no arguing that. And if you really want to feel like you're being hugged by what's on the table in front you, you have to make grandma's recipe. We let this sauce simmer on the stove for hours so the whole house fills up with its smell, but you can just as easily buy something premade. Meaty, cheesy, bubbling, and warm, this lasagna is assembled and baked with love, and it's the only one you will ever need. Serve it with a nice green salad on the side, and grandma will be proud of you for eating your veggies, too.

SERVES 8 TO 10

Kosher salt

1 pound lasagna noodles

1 pound whole-milk ricotta cheese

¼ cup freshly grated Parmesan cheese

2 tablespoons extra-virgin olive oil

2 tablespoons chopped fresh basil

2 teaspoons freshly ground black pepper

6 cups Sunday Sauce (recipe follows) or store-bought meat sauce

1 pound fresh mozzarella, sliced into ¼-inch-thick rounds

Fresh basil leaves, for serving

Preheat the oven to 350°F.

Bring a large pot of salted water to a boil. Cook the noodles until they are just barely al dente, about 5 minutes. Drain and lay the noodles flat on a paper towel to prevent sticking.

In a large bowl, stir together the ricotta, Parmesan, olive oil, basil, pepper, and salt to taste.

In a 9 × 13-inch baking dish, spread 1½ cups of the Sunday sauce on the bottom. Add a single layer of lasagna noodles on top, cutting them as needed to fit. Spread half of the cheese mixture on top. Layer on another 1½ cups of the sauce, then another single layer of lasagna noodles. Add the remaining cheese mixture, then another 1½ cups of the sauce. Top with a final layer of lasagna noodles, then the remaining 1½ cups sauce. Arrange the mozzarella rounds evenly over the top.

Bake until the Sunday sauce is bubbling and the cheese is melted, 45 minutes to 1 hour. Let cool slightly, then sprinkle with fresh basil. Cut into squares and serve.

CONTINUED

Sunday Sauce

MAKES ABOUT 8 CUPS

4 tablespoons extra-virgin olive oil

12 ounces cremini mushrooms, sliced

Kosher salt

1 pound ground beef

2 large yellow onions, diced

3 carrots, finely chopped

3 celery stalks, finely chopped

2 pounds Roma (plum) tomatoes, diced

1 cup red wine

2 (6-ounce) cans tomato paste

2 bay leaves

4 garlic cloves, minced

1 tablespoon onion powder

1 tablespoon freshly ground black pepper, plus more to taste

In a Dutch oven, heat 1 tablespoon of the olive oil over medium heat. Add the mushrooms and cook, undisturbed, until some liquid has released, about 5 minutes. Continue to cook, stirring occasionally, until golden brown, about 5 minutes more. Season with salt and transfer to a bowl.

Add another 1 tablespoon of the olive oil to the Dutch oven. Add the beef, season with salt, and cook over medium heat, breaking it up with a wooden spoon, until browned and cooked through, 7 to 10 minutes. Transfer to the bowl with the mushrooms.

Add the remaining 2 tablespoons olive oil to the Dutch oven. Add the onions and cook over medium heat, stirring occasionally, until translucent, about 5 minutes. Add the carrots, celery, and a pinch of salt. Cook, stirring occasionally, until the vegetables are soft, about 30 minutes, adding splashes of water as needed to prevent burning.

Add the tomatoes and any collected juices, 2 cups water, the wine, tomato paste, and bay leaves. Stir to incorporate the tomato paste.

Return the mushrooms and beef to the pot. Stir in the garlic, onion powder, and pepper. Reduce the heat to low and cook until the sauce is thick and fragrant, 30 to 45 minutes. Season to taste with salt and additional pepper. Discard the bay leaf. Remove the Dutch oven from the heat and let the sauce cool.

Transfer to an airtight container and store in the freezer for up to 3 months.

Sausage and Spinach-Stuffed Pasta Shells

Looking for a deeply satisfying pasta dish? Look no further than this savory mixture of fennel-scented sausage and ricotta. The only thing that could possibly make that combination better is, of course, stuffing it into jumbo shells. They look cool and taste delicious, and nobody will know how easy they were to make.

SERVES 8 TO 10

Kosher salt

1 pound jumbo pasta shells

1 pound hot Italian sausage, casings removed

2 large egg yolks

1½ pounds whole-milk ricotta cheese

½ cups freshly grated Parmesan cheese, plus more for serving

2 cups frozen chopped spinach, thawed, drained, and squeezed dry (see Note)

Freshly ground black pepper

2 cups marinara sauce

8 ounces mozzarella cheese, grated

2 tablespoons extra-virgin olive oil

3 tablespoons fresh basil

Preheat the oven to 350°F.

Bring a large pot of salted water to a boil. Add the shells and cook until just shy of al dente, 2 minutes less than the package directions. Drain.

Meanwhile, in a large skillet, cook the sausage over medium heat, breaking it up with a wooden spoon, until browned, 8 to 10 minutes. Using a slotted spoon, transfer to a large bowl. Let cool slightly. Add the egg yolks, ricotta, Parmesan, and spinach and stir to combine. Season with salt and pepper.

CONTINUED

Pasta and Grains

Spread 1 cup of the marinara sauce in the bottom of a 9 × 13-inch baking dish. Working with one pasta shell at a time, spoon the sausage mixture into the shells. Place the stuffed shells on top of the sauce in the baking dish. Pour the remaining 1 cup sauce over the shells. Sprinkle the mozzarella over the top and drizzle with the olive oil.

Cover with foil and bake until the cheese is melted and golden brown, 15 to 20 minutes.

Let the shells cool slightly and sprinkle with the basil. Serve with more Parmesan cheese on the side.

NOTE: To squeeze the liquid out of thawed spinach, wrap the spinach in a paper towel. Hold the towel over the sink and twist and squeeze to release the moisture. Another option is to use a potato ricer and press down to squeeze the liquid out.

Linguine with Caramelized Onions and Mushrooms

It's a quick weeknight number, but we predict this addictive pasta is one of those low-effort, high-impact dishes that will save you time and time again. The ultraluxe sauce gets its creaminess along with the pleasant surprise of a tang from Greek yogurt, which melds with sweet onions and earthy mushrooms to coat every noodle. Like a little black dress or a solid pair of jeans, this dish can stand on its own or be dressed up—you can just as easily use cremini as you can spring for some special oyster or maitake mushrooms; and while store-bought linguine is the fastest route to yum, if you want to go all out with handmade pasta, we won't stop you. Follow the recipe for Fresh Tagliatelle on page 162 and cut the noodles thinner to make linguine and boil it for about 2 minutes.

SERVES 4

4 tablespoons extra-virgin olive oil

2 large yellow or white onions, thinly sliced

Kosher salt and freshly ground black pepper

1 pound mushrooms, such as cremini, sliced

8 ounces linguine or other long pasta

½ cup plain whole-milk Greek yogurt

Fresh parsley, for serving

In a large skillet, heat 3 tablespoons of the olive oil over medium-high heat. Add the onions, season with salt and pepper, and cook, stirring frequently, until soft and translucent, 2 to 5 minutes. Reduce the heat to medium and continue to cook, stirring occasionally, for another 10 minutes. Add the mushrooms and continue cooking until the onions are caramelized and the mushrooms are golden brown, another 5 to 10 minutes.

Meanwhile, bring a large pot of salted water to a boil. Add the pasta and cook to al dente according to the package directions. Reserving 1 cup of the pasta cooking water, drain the pasta.

Add the pasta and ½ cup of the pasta cooking water to the onions and mushrooms and cook over medium-high heat, tossing to coat, until the pasta is glossy. Remove the skillet from the heat. Stir in the yogurt to coat, adding more water, ¼ cup at a time, as needed to thin the sauce.

To serve, divide the pasta among bowls and top with parsley and pepper.

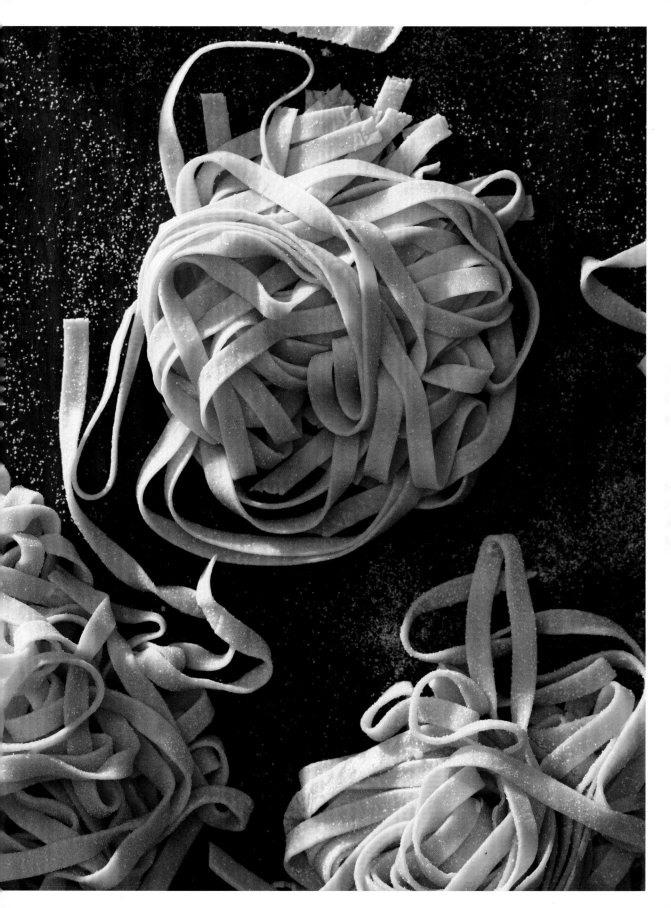

Farro Salad

Simple, light, crunchy, and striking, this salad is one you will make again and again. It's a perfect option for a potluck, a picnic, a summer side, or a savory accompaniment to any meat or fish. Plus, it's endlessly customizable. We like farro for its earthiness and chewy bite, but any hearty grain—think barley, orzo, or rice—makes the perfect base for your favorite veggies and herbs. And the zippy dressing here works with pretty much anything. Make this salad on Sunday and eat it all week long.

SERVES 4 TO 6

1 cup farro

½ cup extra-virgin olive oil

3 tablespoons red wine vinegar

1 teaspoon honey or agave

1 shallot, minced

2 garlic cloves, grated

1 tablespoon grated lemon zest

1 teaspoon kosher salt, plus more to taste

¼ teaspoon freshly ground black pepper, plus more to taste

1 cup diced Persian (mini) or English cucumber

1 cup pitted Castelvetrano or other green olives

½ cup sliced radishes

½ cup chopped fresh parsley

¼ cup roughly chopped fresh dill

In a large pot, combine the farro and 3 cups water. Bring to a boil, then reduce the heat to low and cook until the farro is tender but still has some bite, 20 to 25 minutes. (Use a large spoon to skim foam off the surface as needed.)

Meanwhile, in a large bowl, whisk together the olive oil, vinegar, honey, shallot, garlic, lemon zest, 1 teaspoon salt, and ¼ teaspoon pepper.

Drain the farro and transfer it to the bowl with the dressing. Add the cucumber, olives, radishes, parsley, and dill and toss to combine. Taste and season with additional salt and pepper as desired.

Serve immediately, or store refrigerated in an airtight container for up to 5 days.

Stone-Ground Grits with Scallions and Garlic-Chile Oil

If you're new to grits, welcome—we think you'll like it here. Grits are stone-ground from a type of dried corn called hominy. When they cook in water, they get super creamy and dreamy, and when you toss in some cheese to that, well, you can imagine. Their mild taste is a canvas for flavorful toppings, and so here we have added a healthy dose of spice. Entrees will never be lonely when paired with this savory knockout, and it's just as successful at brunch as it is at dinner. Let's just say grits have never met a protein they didn't love.

SERVES 4 TO 6

½ cup extra-virgin olive oil

6 garlic cloves, thinly sliced

1 Fresno or serrano chile, thinly sliced

2 teaspoons crushed red pepper flakes

Kosher salt

1 cup stone-ground grits

½ cup whole milk

1 cup shredded white cheddar cheese

2 tablespoons unsalted butter

Freshly ground black pepper

In a small saucepan, heat the olive oil over medium heat. Add the garlic, chile, and pepper flakes, stirring constantly until the garlic is golden brown, 2 to 3 minutes. Transfer the garlic-chile oil to a jar and set aside.

In a large saucepan, bring 4 cups water seasoned with 1 teaspoon salt to a boil. Slowly pour in the grits, whisking constantly to prevent any lumps. Reduce the heat to medium-low and cook, stirring constantly, until the water is absorbed, about 10 minutes.

Stir in the milk. Add the cheddar and stir until it has melted and the grits are creamy. Remove the pan from the heat and stir in the butter. Taste and season with additional salt and some black pepper.

Divide among bowls and garnish each with the garlic-chile oil.

Chocolate

Sour Cream Chocolate Tart

Sour cream can be divisive. Some people love it, others hate it . . . and some people who think they hate it are actually okay with it only in their desserts. It has a very specific tang to be sure, and it also makes for a silky, light, and creamy filling in this classic sweet tart shell. Fresh fruit topping or fruit preserves are more than welcome!

MAKES ONE 9-INCH TART

For the crust

¼ cup heavy cream

3 large egg yolks

2¾ cups all-purpose flour, plus more for dusting

2 sticks (8 ounces) unsalted butter, chilled and cut into cubes

¼ cup sugar

¼ teaspoon kosher salt

Softened butter, for greasing

For the filling

1 cup full-fat sour cream

1 large egg yolk

½ cup whole milk

6 ounces bittersweet chocolate, finely chopped

Whipped cream (optional; see Note, page 208), for serving

Chopped nuts (optional)

MAKE THE CRUST: In a small bowl, whisk the cream and egg yolks until smooth.

In a food processor, combine the flour, butter, sugar, and salt and pulse until a coarse meal forms. With the motor running, gradually stream in the cream mixture until just combined.

Turn the dough out onto a lightly floured surface and knead 4 or 5 times to bring the dough together.

Divide the dough in half and shape each half into a 1-inch-thick disk. Layer each disk between two sheets of parchment paper, then wrap in plastic wrap. Chill for at least 30 minutes and up to 2 hours. (You can freeze the unused disk, wrapped and placed in a resealable zip-top bag, for up to 4 months.)

Preheat the oven to 375°F. Grease a 9-inch tart pan.

Chocolate

CONTINUED

Roll out one of the disks to a round ¼ inch thick. Transfer the round to the prepared pan and press the dough evenly up the sides. Trim any excess dough, and poke holes all over the tart shell with the tines of a fork.

Cover the tart shell with a piece of parchment paper and pour pie weights or dried beans into the center. Bake the crust for 20 minutes, remove the paper and pie weights, and continue to bake the crust until lightly golden, about 10 minutes more. Let cool.

Reduce the oven temperature to 350°F.

MAKE THE FILLING: In a medium bowl, whisk the sour cream and egg yolk until smooth.

In a medium saucepan, bring the milk to a gentle boil over medium-low heat. Turn off the heat and add the chocolate, stirring constantly until the chocolate has melted and the mixture is smooth. Slowly add the sour cream mixture and stir to incorporate.

Pour the filling into the cooled crust. Return to the oven and bake until the filling is set, about 25 minutes. Remove and let cool to room temperature, then chill for at least 1 hour before serving.

Top with whipped cream and nuts, if desired.

Chocolate-Orange Cake

Chocolate and orange are one of the most classic pairings around. The light brightness of the citrus is the perfect foil for rich, dense dark chocolate. This cake gets a triple-punch of orange thanks to zest in the batter, juice in the syrup, and more zest on the top of the cake for a final flair.

MAKES ONE 9-INCH CAKE

For the cake

Vegetable oil, for greasing

1 cup all-purpose flour

½ cup dark cacao powder

2 teaspoons baking powder

½ teaspoon kosher salt

1¼ cups sugar

1 cup sour cream or plain whole-milk Greek yogurt

½ cup vegetable oil

3 large eggs

2 teaspoons grated orange zest, plus more for serving

1 cup bittersweet chocolate chips

For the syrup

⅓ cup fresh orange juice

⅓ cup sugar

For the glaze

½ cup heavy cream

¼ cup coarsely chopped bittersweet chocolate or chocolate chips

MAKE THE CAKE: Preheat the oven to 350°F. Grease a 9-inch round cake pan and line the bottom with a round of parchment paper.

Sift the flour, cacao, baking powder, and salt into a medium bowl. Stir in the sugar.

In a large bowl, whisk the sour cream, oil, eggs, and orange zest. Add one-third of the flour mixture, folding gently until smooth. Repeat twice more. Fold in the chocolate chips.

Pour the batter into the prepared pan. Bake until a tester inserted in the center comes out clean, 40 to 50 minutes.

Let the cake cool in the pan for 10 minutes, then invert it onto a wire rack and set the rack inside a sheet pan.

MEANWHILE, MAKE THE SYRUP: In a small saucepan, combine the orange juice and sugar and cook over medium heat, whisking to dissolve the sugar. Boil for 30 seconds, then remove the pan from the heat.

CONTINUED

Use a skewer to poke holes all over the cake. Carefully pour the syrup over the cake and continue to let cool to room temperature.

MAKE THE GLAZE: In a small saucepan, bring the cream to a gentle boil over medium-low heat, then immediately turn off the heat. Add the chocolate chips and stir until the chocolate has melted and the mixture is smooth. Let cool, stirring occasionally, until slightly thickened but still pourable.

Pour the glaze over the cake, letting it drip down the sides. Garnish with additional orange zest before slicing and serving.

Rye Chocolate Chip Cookies

Just when you thought chocolate chip cookies couldn't get any better . . . along comes rye flour, your new best baking friend. Rye flour is known for its deep, nutty taste and soft texture, which thankfully for all of us translates into deeply flavored, thin, and crispy cookies. The best part about this recipe is that you can roll the dough into short logs, store them wrapped in the fridge for a week or the freezer for a couple of months, and slice off and bake one (or more than one) cookie whenever the craving hits.

MAKES 24 COOKIES

1 (12-ounce) bag semisweet or dark chocolate chips

1 cup all-purpose flour

1 cup rye flour

1 teaspoon baking soda

¼ teaspoon kosher salt

2 sticks (8 ounces) unsalted butter, at room temperature

¾ cup granulated sugar

¾ cup packed light brown sugar

2 teaspoons vanilla extract

2 large eggs

Flaky salt

Set aside ¼ cup of chocolate chips.

In a medium bowl, whisk together both flours, the baking soda, and salt.

In a stand mixer fitted with the paddle, beat together the butter and both sugars on low until the mixture is pale and fluffy but still grainy, 4 to 5 minutes, scraping down the sides of the bowl as needed. Beat in the vanilla. Add the eggs, one at a time, beating after each addition. Stir in the flour mixture until just combined and no dry streaks remain (do not overmix). Fold in the remaining chocolate chips.

Divide the dough in half and transfer each half to a sheet of parchment paper or plastic wrap. Use your hands to form each portion of dough into a log about 2 inches in diameter. Wrap the logs in the parchment paper and chill in the refrigerator for at least 1 hour.

Preheat the oven to 350°F. Line two baking sheets with parchment paper.

Use a sharp knife to slice each log into 12 even rounds. Arrange the cookies on the prepared baking sheets 3 inches apart. Top with the reserved chocolate chips and flaky salt.

Bake the cookies for 10 minutes. Rotate the baking sheets front to back, then bake until the cookies are puffed and golden brown, about 4 minutes more.

Chocolate

193

Spiced Chocolate Lava Cake

We can't think of a time when chocolate is ever bad, but we do know that it's extra good when you add a little heat to it. Here cayenne and chili powder give these individual cakes an unexpected pow. These lava babies are decadent treats thanks to a short cooking time that produces a firm exterior and a gooey, melted interior. If you want them more molten, bake for even less time. If you're not about the lava, bake the cakes for an additional minute or two.

MAKES 4 CAKES

Softened butter, for greasing

6 ounces semisweet baking chocolate, roughly chopped

1½ sticks (6 ounces) unsalted butter, cubed, at room temperature

¼ teaspoon cayenne pepper

½ teaspoon ground cinnamon

½ teaspoon ground chili powder

3 large eggs

½ cup granulated sugar

⅓ cup all-purpose flour

Confectioners' sugar, for serving (optional)

Grated orange zest, for serving (optional)

Preheat the oven to 350°F. Grease 4 (6-ounce) ramekins and place them on a sheet pan.

Set a medium saucepan or heatproof bowl over a saucepan of simmering water over low heat, ensuring the top pan (or bowl) does not touch the water directly. Add the chocolate to the top pan and heat, stirring constantly, until completely melted. (Alternatively, melt the chocolate in a small microwave-safe bowl in the microwave in 30-second increments, stirring after each, until melted and smooth.) Stir in the butter, cayenne, cinnamon, and chili powder. Let cool slightly.

In a small bowl, beat the eggs and granulated sugar together until the eggs start to whiten and foam.

While whisking continuously, add 2 tablespoons of the melted chocolate mixture to the egg mixture to warm the eggs. Add the remaining chocolate mixture and flour and stir until the batter is smooth and no dry streaks remain.

Divide the batter among the prepared ramekins. Bake the cakes until just set, about 10 minutes. Immediately invert each ramekin onto a dessert plate. If desired, dust the cakes with confectioners' sugar and orange zest. Serve immediately.

Raw Vegan Chocolate Fudge Brownies

Well, it's possible. Essentially the essence of trail mix with frosting on top, these raw, vegan brownies are packed with protein and just the right amount of natural sweetness. But note, the frosting sets up quickly, so it will need to be used right away. To get the cleanest lines, run a chef's knife under hot water and wipe it with a towel before each cut.

MAKES 16 BROWNIES

1 cup almonds

½ cup pecan halves, plus ½ cup chopped pecans

¾ cup unsweetened raw cacao powder

¼ teaspoon kosher salt

2½ cups pitted dates

For the frosting

1 cup unsweetened raw cacao powder, sifted

¼ cup coconut oil, melted

⅓ cup maple syrup, plus more to taste

1 teaspoon vanilla extract

Kosher salt

Flaky salt, for sprinkling

Line an 8 × 8-inch baking pan with parchment paper, leaving a 1-inch overhang on two sides.

In a food processor, pulse the almonds and the pecan halves together until very finely ground. Add the cacao powder and salt and pulse to combine. Transfer the mixture to a large bowl.

Add the dates to the food processor and pulse until they form a thick paste. Transfer to a separate bowl.

Return the cacao mixture to the food processor and slowly add the date paste until a dough forms.

Transfer the dough to the prepared baking pan and press it into an even layer. Chill until set, 10 to 15 minutes.

MEANWHILE, MAKE THE FROSTING: In a medium bowl, whisk together the cacao powder, coconut oil, maple syrup, vanilla, and a pinch of salt until the mixture is thick and smooth. Taste and adjust the sweetness as needed. Add more maple syrup or coconut oil if it's too thick, or more cacao if it's too thin.

As soon as the brownies are set, use the parchment overhang to lift them out of the pan. Transfer to a cutting board. Working quickly, spread the frosting all over the brownies, using an offset spatula or the back of a spoon to create swirls. Sprinkle the chopped pecans and some flaky salt over the top. Slice the brownies into 16 squares and serve.

Chocolate Banana Pops

This set-it-and-forget-it dessert is easy to make, and a perfect surprise for friends. We like to eat these frozen banana pops on ice pop sticks, but if you don't have any, you can just use your hands—it'll be messier, but every bit as tasty. After you've dipped the bananas in their chocolate shell, feel free to get creative with the toppings and decorations. We love the combination of crushed pistachios and chopped freeze-dried strawberries, but anything that adds crunch and color would be up for the task!

MAKES 8 POPS

4 ripe bananas, peeled and halved crosswise

8 ounces semisweet chocolate chips

2 tablespoons coconut oil

¼ cup almonds, chopped

¼ cup pistachios, chopped

¼ cup freeze-dried strawberries, ground

Line a plate with parchment paper. Insert a wooden pop stick into the cut end of each banana half, pushing it in about halfway up the length. Place the bananas on the lined plate and freeze for at least 30 minutes.

Set a medium saucepan or heatproof bowl over a saucepan of simmering water over low heat, ensuring the top pan (or bowl) does not touch the water directly. Add the chocolate and coconut oil to the top pan and heat, stirring constantly, until completely melted. (Alternatively, melt the chocolate and coconut oil together in a small microwave-safe bowl in the microwave in 30-second increments, stirring after each, until melted and smooth.)

Transfer the chocolate mixture to a tall, heatproof glass. Remove the bananas from the freezer. Holding onto the pop stick, dip each frozen banana into the chocolate mixture to cover completely. Immediately sprinkle on chopped nuts and freezer-dried strawberries. Hold the bananas upright until the chocolate shell has dried, about 30 seconds, then lay them back on the plate.

Enjoy immediately or return the bananas to the freezer to harden completely, 30 minutes to 1 hour.

Vegan Chocolate Cake

Based on a midcentury "ration cake," this recipe uses pantry staples. The leavening of this cake depends on the baking soda combined with two acidic ingredients: natural cocoa powder and vinegar. Make sure you don't substitute Dutch process cocoa (which has been alkalized) for the more acidic natural cocoa powder; and don't use a vinegar with less than 5% acidity. If you'd prefer a layer cake, scale this recipe up, bake in two pans, and stack them!

MAKES ONE 8-INCH SQUARE CAKE

Vegetable oil, for greasing

1½ cups all-purpose flour

1 cup granulated sugar

¼ cup unsweetened natural cocoa powder (not Dutch process)

1 teaspoon baking soda

½ teaspoon kosher salt

⅓ cup vegetable oil

1 tablespoon vinegar, such as apple cider vinegar

1 teaspoon pure vanilla extract

1 tablespoon confectioners' sugar, for serving

Preheat the oven to 350°F. Grease an 8 × 8-inch baking dish with oil.

Sift together the flour, granulated sugar, cocoa powder, baking soda, and salt into a large bowl.

In a liquid measuring cup, combine the oil, vinegar, vanilla, and 1 cup cold water. Add the wet ingredients to the flour mixture and whisk until the batter is smooth.

Pour the batter into the baking dish and bake until a tester inserted into the center of the cake comes out clean, 35 to 40 minutes, rotating the dish after 25 minutes.

Allow the cake to cool in the pan on a wire rack for 20 to 30 minutes. Dust with the confectioners' sugar, slice, and serve.

Chocolate Chip Scones

Handmade scones are an evergreen calling card. They will always make the perfect housewarming gift, breakfast for company, or afternoon tea accompaniment. We love sneaking chocolate into these scones in the form of chocolate chips, which are subtle enough not to dominate the scone entirely and kept in check by the delicate flavors of orange zest. To incorporate an earthy, herbal layer, too, try adding culinary lavender or rosemary.

MAKES 8 SCONES

For the scones

3½ cups all-purpose flour, plus more for dusting

½ teaspoon baking soda

½ teaspoon baking powder

¾ cup sugar

½ teaspoon kosher salt

2 sticks (8 ounces) cold butter, cut into ½-inch-thick slices

1 cup semisweet chocolate chips

Grated zest of 1 orange

1 teaspoon lavender flowers or rosemary (optional

½ cup heavy cream

¾ cup buttermilk (see Notes)

For serving

Softened unsalted butter

¼ cup marmalade or berry jam, such as Strawberry-Chile Jam (page 262)

MAKE THE SCONES: Preheat the oven to 400°F. Line a baking sheet with parchment paper.

In a large bowl, whisk together the flour, baking soda, baking powder, sugar, and salt. Add the cold butter and use your fingertips to incorporate the butter into the flour mixture until the pieces of butter are no bigger than peas and the mixture is crumbly.

Scatter the chocolate chips, orange zest, and lavender (if using) over the flour mixture.

Create a well in the center of the flour mixture. Pour the cream and buttermilk into the well and gently turn the mixture with one hand while holding the bowl in place with the other hand. Continue mixing by hand until a dough forms. Transfer the dough to a floured work surface and pat it into a flat round about 1½ inches thick.

Cut the dough into 8 equal wedges. Gently pull the scones apart and arrange them on the prepared baking sheet, spacing them 1 inch apart.

Bake for 10 minutes. Rotate the baking sheet front to back and continue to bake until the edges and tops are golden, 5 to 8 minutes more. Test for doneness by applying slight pressure on the top of a scone. If the scone yields under the pressure, continue baking for another 3 to 5 minutes.

Serve warm with softened butter and jam alongside.

NOTES: If you don't have buttermilk, stir 2 teaspoons apple cider vinegar or lemon juice into ¾ cup milk and let stand for 5 minutes before using.

Doubling this recipe is a great way to use up buttermilk. You can freeze the scones after cutting them out and before baking. There's no need to thaw them before baking, but you will need to bake them for 5 minutes longer.

Avocado-Chocolate Milkshake

Sure, you might be used to mixing avocado into your green shakes to thicken them up, but what if you mixed them into a chocolate milkshake? Yes, a chocolate milkshake! We love how this dessert (or, really, anytime treat) highlights the sweetness of avocados. Plus, it's a perfect way to use an avocado that's not quite as ripe as you'd like it to be . . . especially when you find that out once you've already cut into it!

SERVES 1

½ young (underripe) avocado

1 cup whole milk

2 tablespoons sugar

½ teaspoon pure vanilla extract

½ cup ice

2 tablespoons chocolate sauce

1 teaspoon chocolate shavings, for serving

Scoop the avocado into a blender. Add the milk, sugar, vanilla, and ice and blend on high until the mixture is smooth.

Place the chocolate sauce in a tall glass and turn to coat the inside. Pour the milkshake into the glass and sprinkle the chocolate shavings on top.

Coconut Cacao Granola

This granola is a great excuse to have chocolate for breakfast. It's a long way away from the sugary chocolate-flavored cereal you might have eaten out of a box when you were growing up. Here, finely ground raw cacao is tossed with shaved coconut, oats, and maple syrup to create delicious, addictive clusters that are decidedly more nutty than sweet. Best of all, you can make a bunch and keep it in an airtight container for up to 2 weeks in your pantry, or 3 months in your freezer.

SERVES 8

1½ cups old-fashioned rolled oats

1½ cups unsweetened coconut flakes

¼ cup ground flaxseed

¼ teaspoon sea salt

¼ cup coconut oil, melted

¼ cup maple syrup

¼ cup unsweetened raw cacao powder

2 tablespoons almond butter

1 teaspoon pure vanilla extract

Preheat the oven to 300°F. Line two baking sheets with parchment paper.

In a large bowl, combine the oats, coconut flakes, ground flaxseed, and salt.

In a medium bowl, stir together the coconut oil, maple syrup, cacao powder, almond butter, and vanilla. Pour the oil mixture over the oat mixture and toss, stirring to coat completely.

Divide the granola between the two baking sheets, spreading it into an even layer. Bake for 10 minutes, then remove from the oven to stir and flip any large clusters. Bake until the granola is golden and crispy, 10 to 15 minutes more. Let cool.

Salted Chocolate Tahini Milkshake

If you're one of those people with more of a savory tooth than a sweet tooth, this decadent treat is for you. Think of it as an adult Reese's peanut butter cup in a glass—except we've swapped the peanut butter for tahini, which is made from ground sesame seeds. If you choose to include maca powder, which you can easily find at natural foods stores and online, you'll taste some earthiness, too. The tahini and chocolate ice cream are the most important ingredients here—and you could make a shake with nothing more.

SERVES 1 OR 2

½ cup whole milk

2 pitted Medjool dates

1 pint chocolate ice cream

¼ cup tahini

2 teaspoons unsweetened raw cacao powder (optional)

2 teaspoons maca powder (optional)

Optional toppings

Whipped cream (see Note)

Cacao nibs

Flaky salt

In a blender, combine the milk and dates and blend on high speed until smooth, but still thick.

Add the ice cream, tahini, and cacao powder and/or maca (if using) and blend again until well incorporated. Pour the milkshake into glasses and serve immediately with desired toppings.

NOTE: Make your own whipped cream by whisking together—by hand or with an electric mixer—¼ cup heavy cream with 2 teaspoons sugar until doubled in volume. This will give you about ½ cup.

More Sweet Treats

Citrus Buttermilk Cake

Buttermilk isn't used nearly enough in cake baking, in our opinion, since it adds a light springiness to a flavorful, simple crumb, where milk or cream can be dense or rich. Don't sleep on the lemon and orange syrup that soaks the cake after it's baked, nor the lemon and orange glaze—it's the last step in the citrus trifecta here, which might even help this cake meet your body's vitamin C requirements for a single day.

MAKES ONE 8-INCH SQUARE CAKE

Softened butter, for greasing

1¼ cups all-purpose flour

1¼ teaspoons baking powder

¼ teaspoon baking soda

¼ teaspoon kosher salt

2 large eggs

1 cup granulated sugar

½ teaspoon pure vanilla extract

4 tablespoons unsalted butter, melted

¾ cup buttermilk

3 teaspoons grated lemon zest

2 teaspoons grated orange zest

For the syrup

3 tablespoons confectioners' sugar

1 tablespoon fresh orange juice

1 tablespoon fresh lemon juice

For the glaze

¾ cup confectioners' sugar

1 tablespoon buttermilk

1 tablespoon unsalted butter, melted

1 teaspoon fresh orange juice

1 teaspoon fresh lemon juice

Lemon slices and/or zest, for serving (optional)

Orange slices and/or zest, for serving (optional)

Preheat the oven to 350°F. Lightly butter an 8 × 8-inch baking dish and line with parchment paper, leaving a 1-inch overhang on two sides. Butter the parchment.

In a medium bowl, whisk together the flour, baking powder, baking soda, and salt.

In a large bowl, whisk together the eggs, granulated sugar, vanilla, melted butter, buttermilk, lemon zest, and orange zest until smooth. Add the flour mixture and stir until just incorporated and no dry streaks remain.

Pour the batter into the baking dish. Bake until the cake is golden brown and a tester inserted into the center comes out clean, 25 to 35 minutes.

MEANWHILE, MAKE THE SYRUP: In a small bowl, whisk together the confectioners' sugar, orange juice, and lemon juice until smooth.

Remove the cake from the oven and let cool for 5 minutes. Poke holes all over the top of the cake with the tines of a fork. Slowly drizzle the syrup over the cake and let cool completely.

MEANWHILE, MAKE THE GLAZE: In a small bowl, whisk together the confectioners' sugar, buttermilk, melted butter, orange juice, and lemon juice until smooth.

Use the parchment overhang to lift the cake out of the pan and transfer it to a serving plate. Pour the glaze slowly and evenly over the cake and let sit for about 2 minutes, until the glaze is dry and set. Garnish with additional lemon and orange slices and zest, if desired, before slicing.

Baklava

Baklava, a classic dessert in Middle Eastern cuisines, is a delicious treat made with flaky pastry, honey, and nuts. You'll need a napkin after crunching through these buttery layers of sticky, textured goodness. When working with phyllo dough, remember to be fast. Five layers is traditional, but we like three because it means one box of phyllo (plus a higher filling-to-flake ratio). If you can't find May Zahar (orange blossom water), you can also use super finely chopped orange and/or lemon zest, just remember to strain it out at the end. These taste just like grandma's—but we won't tell her if you play around with some variations on the original. Switch up the three main elements (the nuts, the honey, and the syrup) to experiment with different flavors.

MAKES 90 PIECES

Softened margarine, ghee, or clarified butter, for greasing

7 cups pistachios, crushed or finely chopped, plus more as needed

1 tablespoon ground cinnamon, plus more to taste

1 cup packed light brown sugar

¾ cup honey, plus more as needed

1 teaspoon plus 2 tablespoons May Zahar (orange blossom water)

1 (1-pound) package (9 × 14-inch) frozen phyllo dough, thawed

1½ cups (12 ounces) melted unsalted margarine, ghee, or clarified butter (see Note)

1 cup granulated sugar

Position a rack in the center of the oven and preheat the oven to 375°F. Grease a large sheet pan.

In a large bowl, stir together the pistachios, cinnamon, brown sugar, and honey. Stir in 1 teaspoon of the May Zahar. The mixture should be sticky enough to hold together in clusters, but not runny. (If it's too wet, add more nuts; if it's too dry and crumbling apart, add more honey.)

Gently lay out one sheet of phyllo (keep the rest covered so it doesn't dry out). Brush with 1 teaspoon of the melted margarine. Lay a second sheet of phyllo over the top and drizzle and brush with another 1 teaspoon margarine. Repeat again to create a third layer. (Work

CONTINUED

carefully, as phyllo tears easily. If it tears, just brush the piece back into place; the layers will cover any holes.) Spread ½ cup of the nut filling along one long side, about ¼ inch in from the edge. Roll up the nut filling in the layers of phyllo to create a log. Place the log on the prepared sheet pan, seam-side down; it should fit perfectly along the shorter edge of the pan.

Continue working with the remaining phyllo, margarine, and filling to create 14 logs total. Brush the logs with the remaining melted margarine. Use a pastry scraper or sharp knife to slice the logs crosswise into 1-inch rounds. Make sure to cut them all the way through, but leave them touching each other in a log shape.

Bake until the top layer is crisp and flaky and the baklava is golden brown all over, 20 to 40 minutes. Check every 10 minutes; if it is browning too quickly, reduce the heat.

Meanwhile, in a medium saucepan, combine the granulated sugar and ½ cup water and cook over medium heat, whisking constantly, until rolling bubbles appear, about 3 minutes. Reduce the heat to low and add the remaining 2 tablespoons May Zahar. Continue to cook, stirring occasionally, until the syrup is thick and slowly drizzles off a spoon, about 15 minutes. This step is the most important—if the syrup is too watery, it will make the baklava mushy. If it is too sticky, it will coat the baklava unevenly, harden, and make it impossible to bite. Stir in a pinch of cinnamon, if desired. Reduce the heat to low to keep warm.

Remove the baklava from the oven and immediately spoon a thin layer of syrup onto one of the edge pieces; it should sit on top of the baklava. If it sinks in and absorbs, return the syrup to low heat to thicken a bit further.

When the correct texture has been achieved, spoon the syrup over all the baklava and set aside to cool before serving.

Store the baklava wrapped in plastic wrap or parchment paper for 1 to 2 weeks at room temperature, in the refrigerator for up to 6 weeks, or in the freezer for up to 6 months.

NOTE: Whatever you do, don't use regular unclarified butter here. You need something without milk solids—they'll burn in the oven.

Coconut Flan

Flan, which the French call crème caramel, is a rich, creamy custard popular in Spain and many Latin American countries. When it's inverted before serving, a showstopping gooey caramel sauce is revealed. (We recommend using a platter with a lip to keep all that goodness from running off the edges.) We've riffed on this beloved classic with a sweet and smooth twist, adding a coconut triple-threat. Coconut milk, sweetened condensed coconut milk, and toasted coconut flakes? Yes, yes, and yes again.

MAKES ONE 9-INCH FLAN

1 cup sugar

3 cups full-fat coconut milk

1 cup sweetened condensed coconut milk (see Note)

½ teaspoon kosher salt

1 teaspoon almond extract

5 large eggs

5 large egg yolks

Hot water

½ cup unsweetened coconut flakes, toasted, for serving

Preheat the oven to 325°F. Set a 9-inch cake pan or pie plate inside a roasting pan.

In a small saucepan, combine ½ cup of the sugar and 3 tablespoons water and bring to a boil over medium heat—do not stir. Cook, undisturbed, until the caramel is deep copper. Pour the mixture into the cake pan, tilting the pan so the caramel coats the bottom. Return the cake pan to the roasting pan and let the caramel cool slightly.

In a medium saucepan, combine the coconut milk, sweetened condensed coconut milk, and the remaining ½ cup sugar. Cook over medium heat, stirring, until the sugar has dissolved, 3 to 4 minutes. Watch carefully so the mixture does not boil over. Remove the saucepan from the heat and stir in the salt and almond extract. Let cool slightly.

CONTINUED

In a large heatproof bowl, whisk the whole eggs and egg yolks until smooth. Add ½ cup of the hot milk mixture to the eggs, whisking constantly, to warm the eggs. Once the egg mixture is warm, stream in the remaining milk mixture and whisk to combine. Strain the milk mixture through a fine-mesh sieve into the cake pan to cover the caramel.

Transfer the roasting pan to a pulled-out oven rack. Pour enough hot water into the roasting pan to come as high up the sides of the cake pan as possible.

Bake until the flan is fully set but jiggles slightly in the middle, 45 minutes to 1 hour.

Remove the flan from the oven and let cool for about 30 minutes, then cover with plastic wrap and refrigerate for at least 6 hours or up to 24 hours.

To serve, run a knife around the edge of the flan before inverting it onto a large platter. Top with the toasted coconut and serve immediately.

NOTE: We use sweetened condensed coconut milk in this mixture for its rich and creamy coconut flavor—it packs a concentrated punch. If you can't find it, regular sweetened condensed milk will work, too.

Coffee Crème Brûlée

Crème brûlée is a luxurious, creamy, decadent dessert with a signature brittle top. Nothing is more fun than cracking through that caramelized sugar to get to the good stuff underneath. We've put a twist on the classic by incorporating ground coffee—use your favorite kind—for some extra flavor and serving it in mini mason jars for extra points on presentation.

SERVES 6

5 large egg yolks

⅓ cup plus ¼ cup sugar

2 cups heavy cream

2 tablespoons medium-ground coffee beans

1 teaspoon pure vanilla extract

½ teaspoon kosher salt

Boiling water

NOTE: The method calls for a kitchen torch at the end. If you don't have one, you can broil for a few minutes instead, but use the ceramic ramekins, not mason jars, since they won't hold up to the broiler heat.

Position a rack in the center of the oven and preheat the oven to 300°F.

In a large bowl, whisk the egg yolks and ⅓ cup of the sugar until just smooth.

In a medium saucepan, heat the cream over low heat. When bubbles appear around the edges, add the coffee and remove from the heat. Stir in the vanilla and salt. Let steep for 3 minutes.

Strain the cream mixture through a fine-mesh sieve into a liquid measuring cup or medium bowl. Immediately temper the eggs by slowly pouring ¼ cup of the hot cream into them, whisking continuously until the cream is incorporated. Transfer the yolk mixture to the remaining cream mixture and whisk again to combine.

Divide the mixture among six 4-ounce mason jars (or ramekins) and place them in a large baking dish. Transfer the baking dish to a pulled-out oven rack and pour in enough boiling water to go three-quarters of the way up the sides of the jars.

Bake until the custard is slightly set but still jiggly in the center, 35 to 40 minutes. Remove the jars and let cool for 20 minutes. Cover the jars and refrigerate for at least 4 hours, or up to 5 days to chill.

Remove the jars from the refrigerator and uncover. Set them in a warm water bath in a large baking dish once more. Sprinkle 2 teaspoons of sugar evenly over the top of each custard. Use a kitchen torch to heat the sugar until it has browned and has formed a crisp layer on the top of the custard. Let cool slightly before serving.

Lemon Bundt Cake

Is there anything more classic than a lemon Bundt? Bright and tart, yet rich and super moist thanks to the addition of Greek yogurt, it almost couldn't get any better . . . until you finish it with a vanilla glaze. This cake is perfect for brunch or dessert—any time you want to signal it's time for spring.

SERVES 10 TO 12

Butter and flour, for the pan

2 cups granulated sugar

2 sticks (8 ounces) unsalted butter, at room temperature

¼ cup heavy cream

6 large eggs

⅓ cup fresh lemon juice

1 teaspoon vanilla extract

3 cups all-purpose flour

1 cup plain whole-milk Greek yogurt

2 tablespoons grated lemon zest

1 tablespoon baking powder

2 teaspoons baking soda

1 teaspoon kosher salt

For the vanilla glaze

1 cup confectioners' sugar

3 tablespoons heavy cream, plus more as needed

1 vanilla bean, split lengthwise

Lemon zest, for serving

Preheat the oven to 350°F. Butter and flour a 12-cup Bundt pan.

In a stand mixer fitted with the paddle, beat together the granulated sugar, butter, and cream on medium speed until light and fluffy, about 4 minutes. Add the eggs, one at a time, beating after each addition to make sure each egg is incorporated. Add the lemon juice and vanilla and continue to beat to incorporate.

Add about one-quarter of the flour, ¼ cup of the yogurt, the lemon zest, baking powder, baking soda, and salt. Continue to beat on medium speed until incorporated. Add the remaining flour and yogurt in three more batches, alternating and making sure the mixture is just combined and not overmixed.

Pour the batter into the prepared pan, spreading it out evenly. Tap the pan against the work surface to make sure it is leveled and free of air pockets.

Bake until a tester inserted in the center of the cake comes out clean, 55 to 60 minutes.

Let cool for 20 minutes in the pan, then invert the cake onto a serving plate.

MEANWHILE, MAKE THE GLAZE: In a small bowl, whisk together the confectioners' sugar and heavy cream. Scrape in the vanilla seeds and whisk in. Add more heavy cream as needed to reach a thin, pourable consistency.

Pour the glaze over the cake and sprinkle with lemon zest. Slice and serve.

Walnut Linzer Cookies with Jam Filling

These cookies are such a pretty treat, and they're especially wonderful as an addition to holiday cookie spreads or gift boxes—but if you're keeping them to yourself, they're perfect with a cup of afternoon tea. These are super customizable so feel free to experiment with different jams, even several at a time, to create a vibrant look. Store-bought jams are totally fair game here, or you can use your own homemade. If you find yourself whipping up a batch of Strawberry-Chile Jam (page 262), just skip the chile for this occasion. Peach jam would also be delicious, as would a pinch of cinnamon added to the cookie batter. If you have a linzer cookie cutter, use it to create half the cookies with cut-out "windows"; if not, use small cutters or a sharp knife to create your own cutouts.

MAKES ABOUT 10 COOKIE SANDWICHES

¾ cup walnuts, toasted

2 cups all-purpose flour, plus more for dusting

½ teaspoon baking powder

3 tablespoons confectioners' sugar, plus more for finishing

¼ teaspoon coarse sea salt

8 tablespoons (1 stick) unsalted butter, at room temperature

¼ cup granulated sugar

1 large egg

½ teaspoon pure vanilla extract

¾ cup jam of your choice

In a food processor, pulse the walnuts until finely chopped. Transfer to a medium bowl and add the flour, baking powder, confectioners' sugar, and salt and stir to combine.

In a stand mixer fitted with the paddle, beat the butter and granulated sugar on medium-high speed until the mixture is light and fluffy. Add the egg and beat until smooth, then add the vanilla. Add the walnut mixture and mix until just combined.

Divide the dough in half and transfer to a work surface. Use your hands to pat each portion of dough into a disk, wrap the disks in plastic wrap, and refrigerate until firm, at least 1 hour or overnight.

CONTINUED

Preheat the oven to 375°F. Line two sheet pans with parchment paper.

Remove the dough from the refrigerator and let sit for 10 minutes. On a lightly floured piece of parchment paper, roll out the dough disks to an ⅛-inch thickness. Transfer the dough to the freezer to chill for 15 minutes (don't skip this step—freezing will allow for precise cutting later).

Using a 2- to 2½-inch cookie cutter, cut an even number of cookies with and without windows from the dough and place them on the prepared sheet pans. Return the cookies to the freezer once again and chill for 15 minutes more.

Bake the cookies until just golden, about 10 minutes. Let cool slightly on the pan, then carefully transfer the cookies to a wire rack to cool completely.

To assemble, place a sheet of parchment paper on a work surface and arrange half of the cookies (the ones without the window cut-outs) on the paper. Use an offset spatula to spread the jam on the cookies and transfer them back to the wire rack. Move the remaining cookies (the ones with the window cut-outs) onto the paper. Dust the top cookies with confectioners' sugar and stack them on top of the bottom cookies to make sandwiches.

Linzer cookies are best within the first 24 hours of baking but will keep at room temperature in an airtight container for up to 2 days.

Mango Sticky Rice

This beloved Thai dessert gets a shower of crispy toasted coconut chips and fried mung beans, a type of legume used in both sweet and savory dishes in many parts of Asia. You can easily find fried moong dal (mung beans) at Indian grocery shops. Though these toppings are great for adding finishing crunch and extra texture, they are not totally necessary. Cashews or pistachios also work beautifully. Look for cartons of 100% coconut milk instead of canned coconut milk, which contains additives.

SERVES 4

1 cup Thai sweet rice (glutinous rice) or Thai black sweet rice

Boiling water, as needed

1½ cups 100% pure coconut milk, such as Aroy-D (see headnote)

¼ cup sugar, plus more to taste

¾ teaspoon kosher salt

2 mangoes (6 to 8 ounces each)

¼ cup coconut chips, toasted (optional)

1 to 2 tablespoons fried mung beans (optional)

Sesame seeds, for garnish (optional)

In a large bowl, combine the rice and 2 cups water. Soak the rice for 8 to 12 hours, adding more water as needed to keep it covered.

Drain the soaked rice in a fine-mesh sieve and rinse it under running water, stirring with your hands, until the water runs clear. Transfer the rice to a steamer insert (see Note).

In a pot just slightly larger in diameter than the steamer insert, bring 2 inches of water to a boil. Set the steamer insert of rice on the pot over the boiling water and cover. Reduce the heat to medium so the water maintains a gentle boil and steam the rice for 25 minutes.

Carefully remove the lid and use a large spoon or paddle to turn the rice over in sections. Add more boiling water to the pot as needed to maintain 2 inches. Cover and continue to steam until the rice is cooked through when you bite into it, another 20 to 30 minutes. Remove the steamer insert from the pot and set aside on a plate.

More Sweet Treats

CONTINUED

Discard any remaining hot water from the pot. Add the coconut milk, sugar, and salt to the pot and cook over medium heat, stirring constantly, until the sugar is dissolved and the liquid is simmering, about 5 minutes. Ladle about ¼ cup of the coconut milk mixture into a small bowl.

Return the rice to the pot and stir to coat with the coconut milk. The mixture should resemble a thick porridge. Cover, reduce the heat to low, and cook the rice for 5 minutes more, stirring once halfway through. Taste the rice for sweetness and add more sugar as desired. Remove the pot from the heat and let the rice rest, covered, until the liquid is absorbed, 15 to 20 minutes.

Meanwhile, use a vegetable peeler to remove the peel on one side of each mango, then set the fruit down, peeled-side up, on a cutting board. Using a paring knife, cut the peeled side of each mango, parallel to the natural curve at the base of the fruit, into 5 or 6 slices 1 inch thick. Hold the mango steady with one hand, fingertips just below the pit, as you make a horizontal cut just above the pit to release the slices.

Repeat with the other sides of the mangoes.

To serve, divide the rice among plates and top each serving with the sliced mango. Drizzle the reserved coconut sauce over each. If desired, sprinkle with toasted coconut, fried mung beans, and sesame seeds (if using).

NOTE: If you do not have a steamer basket set, you can create a similar setup with some basic kitchen equipment. You'll need a fine mesh strainer or colander without plastic parts that can hold the rice over 2 inches of boiling water in a pot with a fitted lid. (Make sure there is at least 2 inches of space between the water level and where the bottom of the steamer or strainer will eventually be placed.)

Passion Fruit Mousse

Surely you've had chocolate mousse. Maybe you've even had a savory mousse, like salmon. Now it's time to meet passion fruit mousse: creamy and decadent, this stunning dessert hits that perfect sweet (and sour—in a good way) spot of sharp and refreshing. This one scores high marks in how easy it is to make as compared to how fancy it sounds.

SERVES 6

¾ cup frozen passion fruit puree, thawed

1½ cups heavy cream

¾ cup sweetened condensed milk

1 teaspoon fresh lime juice

1 teaspoon pure vanilla extract

Kosher salt

Pulp of 3 passion fruits

In a blender, combine the passion fruit puree, cream, sweetened condensed milk, lime juice, vanilla, and a pinch of salt. Blend until smooth, creamy, and thick, about 1 minute.

Divide the mixture evenly among six small ramekins. Cover with plastic wrap, pressing it directly onto the surface to avoid a skin forming. Refrigerate for at least 6 hours or overnight to chill.

Serve the mousse topped with fresh passion fruit pulp.

Rose Water Mixed Berry Trifles

Fluffy, colorful layers of berries, toasted almonds, and rich, creamy pudding—and if that wasn't enough, it's all infused with the fresh, floral beauty that is Turkish rose water, an ingredient used in both savory and sweet dishes throughout the Middle East. It's the star here, and worth getting your hands on, though the quality and sweetness can vary among brands. Our favorite is Cortas—if yours is syrupy or extremely fragrant, add 1 teaspoon at a time, as too much could overpower the dish. We love to serve this delicate treat with mint tea.

SERVES 6 TO 8

For the rose water pudding

2 cups whole milk

2 cups heavy cream

⅔ cup granulated sugar

2 tablespoons cornstarch

2 tablespoons pure rose water

Sea salt

For the trifles

1 quart strawberries, hulled and sliced

2 pints raspberries

1 pint blueberries

Juice of 1 lemon

2 tablespoons granulated sugar

2 cups heavy cream

⅓ cup confectioners' sugar

1 teaspoon almond extract

36 ladyfingers

For serving

Strawberries, raspberries, and blueberries, for garnish

½ cup roasted unsalted almonds, roughly chopped

1 tablespoon dried rose petals (optional)

MAKE THE PUDDING: In a large heavy-bottomed saucepan, combine 1¾ cups of the milk, the cream, and granulated sugar. Bring to a boil over medium heat, stirring occasionally and watching closely to ensure the mixture doesn't boil over. Reduce the heat to a simmer and continue to cook, stirring occasionally to prevent burning, until slightly reduced, 25 to 35 minutes.

In a small bowl or liquid measuring cup, whisk the cornstarch into the remaining ¼ cup milk. Pour the mixture into the pudding and increase the heat to medium. Continue to cook, stirring constantly, until the mixture has thickened, 2 to 3 minutes.

Remove the pan from the heat and stir in the rose water and a pinch of sea salt. Pour the pudding mixture into a 9 × 13-inch baking dish and cover with plastic wrap, pressing it directly onto the surface of the pudding to avoid a skin forming. Refrigerate for at least 20 minutes to chill.

MEANWHILE, PREPARE THE TRIFLES: In a large bowl, combine the strawberries, raspberries, blueberries, lemon juice, and granulated sugar and toss to coat. Let the fruit macerate for 30 minutes.

In a medium bowl, vigorously whisk the cream and confectioners' sugar until soft peaks form. (Alternatively, whip the cream and sugar in a stand mixer fitted with the whisk.) Fold in the almond extract.

Layer half of the ladyfingers into the bottom of six to eight highball glasses, breaking them apart as needed to fit. Spoon in half of the macerated fruit and juices. Divide the rose water pudding evenly among the glasses. Top the pudding with the remaining ladyfingers, then the remaining fruit. Finish with the whipped cream, dividing evenly. Refrigerate the trifles for at least 3 hours or overnight to chill.

TO SERVE: Garnish the trifles with fresh berries, roasted almonds, and dried rose petals (if using).

Cardamom Peach Cobbler with Honey Cream

A cobbler is one of our favorite desserts. It has some traits of a pie, and some of a pudding, too . . . all we know is that when you combine certain things and bake them together, the outcome is going to be fantastic. Peaches get a sort of reverse cobbler treatment here, with the biscuit-like crust on the bottom rather than on top. It's a perfect way to celebrate the peak summertime fruit—but with an infusion of cardamom, a spice from the ginger family. Rye flour adds an earthiness, and the honey cream on top lends just the right amount of sweetness.

SERVES 6 TO 8

4 ripe medium peaches, sliced

1 tablespoon dark brown sugar

½ teaspoon ground cinnamon

8 tablespoons (1 stick) unsalted butter

5 cardamom pods

1½ cups bread flour

½ cup rye flour

1 tablespoon baking powder

1 teaspoon sea salt

2 cups whole milk

1 teaspoon pure vanilla extract

1 tablespoon honey

1 cup heavy cream

Preheat the oven to 375°F.

In a medium bowl, toss the peaches, brown sugar, and cinnamon together. Set aside to macerate.

In a 9-inch cast-iron skillet, melt the butter over medium heat. Add the whole cardamom pods and cook, stirring occasionally, until they are fragrant and the butter is slightly browned, about 5 minutes. Remove the skillet from the heat and let cool slightly.

In a large bowl, whisk together both flours, the baking powder, and sea salt to combine. Add the milk and vanilla and whisk until just combined.

Discard the cardamom pods, leaving the melted butter in the skillet. Pour the batter into the skillet. Evenly top with the peaches and their collected juices.

Bake until the cobbler is puffed and golden brown, 35 to 45 minutes.

Meanwhile, in a medium bowl, whisk together the honey and cream until smooth.

Serve the cobbler with the honey-cream alongside.

Banana-Walnut Bread Pudding

Bread pudding is vastly underrated in the dessert world—often over-looked with so many cakes, cookies, and cobblers all around. But it's crazy yummy, especially with the right mix-ins. Here, walnuts and bananas both inside and on top add a nice crunch to the creamy pudding, but you can use another nut if you prefer. A little whipped cream on the side wouldn't hurt, either (make your own; see Note on page 208). It's also a great way to use up stale bakery bread, whether it's brioche like we use here, or a challah, or your own homemade sourdough (see page 243). You can assemble and bake the bread pudding in as little as 1 hour, but you can also bake it a day ahead. Cool, cover, refrigerate, and warm in a 350°F oven for 15 minutes before serving.

SERVES 6 TO 8

Softened butter, for greasing

2 large eggs

2 cups whole milk

½ cup heavy cream

½ cup sugar

1 teaspoon ground cinnamon

1 loaf brioche, torn into large pieces

1 cup chopped walnuts

2 bananas, sliced on the diagonal

Caramel sauce, for serving (optional)

Preheat the oven to 350°F. Butter a 9 × 13-inch baking dish.

In a large bowl, whisk together the eggs, milk, cream, sugar, and cinnamon until smooth. Add the bread and toss, gently squeezing the bread so it absorbs the liquid. Let soak for 15 minutes.

Add half the bread mixture to the prepared baking dish. Sprinkle with ½ cup of the walnuts and arrange half the bananas on top. Add the remaining bread mixture, sprinkle with the remaining ½ cup walnuts, and arrange the remaining bananas on top.

Bake until the pudding is puffed and lightly golden, about 45 minutes. Let cool slightly before serving.

Simple Lemon Apple Cake

Easy, peasy, lemon-squeezy, as the saying goes . . . and this cake is certainly no exception. This perfect celebration of fall's favorite fruit gets a hit of brightness from lemon juice. You can use any warming spice your heart desires here—cinnamon, cloves, nutmeg, and cardamom are all fair game—even a combination. And if you like, you can convert this cake to muffins since the batter will be enough to fill a standard 12-muffin tin.

MAKES ONE 10-INCH CAKE

Softened butter, for greasing

1½ pounds firm apples, such as Pink Lady, diced (about 4 cups)

¼ cup fresh lemon juice

2 cups all-purpose flour

1 teaspoon baking soda

½ teaspoon kosher salt

½ teaspoon ground cloves, nutmeg, cinnamon, or cardamom

1 cup vegetable oil

2 large eggs, at room temperature

2 cups packed light brown sugar

Grated zest of 1 lemon

1 teaspoon pure vanilla extract

2 tablespoons unsalted butter, melted

Position a rack in the center of the oven and preheat the oven to 350°F. Grease a 10-inch round cake pan (or a 9 × 13-inch baking dish) with butter.

In a large bowl, toss the apples with the lemon juice. In a medium bowl, whisk together the flour, baking soda, salt, and cloves. In another large bowl, whisk together the oil and eggs.

In a small bowl, combine the brown sugar and lemon zest and use your fingers to rub the zest into the grains of sugar. Set aside ¼ cup of the lemon sugar. Gradually add the remaining lemon sugar to the egg mixture. Stir in the vanilla.

Gently fold half of the flour mixture into the egg mixture until just combined. Add the remaining flour mixture and fold until no dry streaks remain.

Fold half of the apples into the batter and pour the batter into the baking dish. Use the back of a spoon or an offset spatula to smooth out the top. Pour the remaining apples on top and sprinkle with the reserved lemon sugar. Drizzle with the melted butter.

Bake the cake for 30 minutes. Rotate the baking dish front to back and bake until a tester inserted into the center comes out clean or with a few dry crumbs, 10 to 15 minutes more.

Preservation and Fermentation

Rosemary-Honey Sourdough Loaf

Mastering the art of bread making is a journey, and you learn as much from the failures as you do from the successes. This is a beginner's sourdough recipe—using starter that you can learn about on page 245—with a few flourishes to get you excited. We're probably not the first ones to tell you that making bread is a multistep, sometimes multiday process, but the warm, comforting scents of honey, rosemary, and garlic wafting up from this loaf as you cut into it will be a sweet, worthwhile reward. Congratulations, bread master!

MAKES 1 SOURDOUGH LOAF

½ cup sourdough starter (see page 245), after peak rise

1 teaspoon chopped fresh rosemary

2 teaspoons kosher salt

2 tablespoons honey

2 garlic cloves, minced

3 cups bread flour, plus more for dusting

Extra-virgin olive oil, for greasing (optional)

Pour the starter into a liquid measuring cup once it has just finished metabolizing a feeding and is starting to go hungry. Add 1 cup warm water and stir to combine, then pour the mixture into a large bowl.

Add the rosemary, salt, honey, garlic, and bread flour to the starter mixture and use your hands to combine well. Continue to knead the dough in the bowl until a rough, shaggy dough ball forms, about 5 minutes. Cover the bowl with a damp kitchen towel and set in a warm place for 30 minutes to rise. You'll see signs of fermentation, like an increase in volume and bubbling along the top of the dough.

Fill a small bowl with warm water. Dip your hands in the water and begin to stretch and fold the dough. Use one hand to pull the dough up, stretching it slightly, then fold the dough back down onto itself, rotating 90 degrees after each stretch. It is helpful to use your other hand to hold on to the dough in the bowl. Set the bowl aside again,

CONTINUED

covered with a damp towel in a warm place, and let the dough rest for 30 minutes again. Repeat the stretching process above, then set the bowl aside once more for another 30 minutes.

Line a high-sided medium bowl with a large dry kitchen towel and dust generously with flour. Gently transfer the dough to a floured surface. Use your hands to gently shape the dough into a round loaf, then turn the loaf upside down and transfer to the prepared bowl. Cover with the overhang of the towel. Transfer to the refrigerator and proof for at least 12 hours or up to 18 hours.

Position a rack in the center of the oven and place a lidded Dutch oven on the rack. Preheat the oven to 450°F for at least 30 minutes.

Remove the proofed bread from the refrigerator. Place a large sheet of parchment over the bowl and carefully invert it to release the dough onto the parchment. Score the top of the loaf with a sharp knife in any pattern you choose; make sure the cuts are at least ¾ inch deep. (If the dough sticks to the knife, dip the blade in olive oil as needed.)

Carefully remove the Dutch oven from the oven and open the lid. Use the parchment to carefully lower the dough (and the parchment) into the Dutch oven. Cover and return to the oven. Bake until the dough has risen, about 25 minutes. Uncover the Dutch oven and continue baking until the crust is deep golden brown, 15 to 20 minutes more.

Remove from the oven. Use the parchment paper to transfer the loaf to a wire rack and let cool completely, at least 2 hours, before slicing. Store the loaf in a bread bag for up to 3 days or in an airtight container in the freezer for up to 3 months.

A Guide to Sourdough Starters

Ah, sourdough starters . . . friend to many, giver of superior loaves, subject of countless memes and online forums. The devotees might gawk at those who have not yet given their lives to these fermented beings ("Did you even live through 2020?"), feeding them (and naming them) as if they were pets. It can be a challenging process, but patience is the biggest key to success, and the results can be endlessly rewarding.

Equipment

Two 1- or 2-quart containers (yogurt or deli containers work great)

Cheesecloth or a small kitchen towel

Rubber band

Ingredients

5 pounds organic bread flour

Filtered water

In a 1- or 2-quart container, combine 1 cup of the bread flour with ½ cup filtered water. Stir until the water is fully incorporated into the flour and no dry streaks remain. It should resemble a thick pancake batter; you might need to add a bit more water to reach the right consistency.

Cover the container with cheesecloth and secure a rubber band over the top. To allow the fermentation to progress as quickly as possible, place the container in a warm place, such as near the oven or a heater. (Around 90°F is an ideal temperature for this part of the process.) It will usually take 24 to 48 hours to see some action in your starter. You are looking for small bubbles to form. If you are using a clear container, check the sides and top for bubbles. Getting the first bubbles to form can be the hardest part, sometimes taking up to 4 days.

Once your starter has begun to bubble, it is officially alive and it's time to start feeding it. To feed your starter, remove all but about ½ cup from the container—just eyeball it. (You can discard what you remove, save it to use in a recipe such as Sourdough Starter Discard Crepes on page 249, or give it to a friend.) Add ½ cup of the bread flour and ¼ cup warm water to the starter in the container. Stir to mix well, then very slowly add more flour or warm water as needed to reach the same pancake batter consistency again. (Do not use cold water here, as it will shock the live cultures.)

Cover the container again and return it to a warm place. Let the starter do its magic again and check on it after 12 hours. If it has risen a bit but started to fall back down, it is time for another feeding. It may need 24 hours to metabolize the flour from the first feeding, usually due to temperature. Over time, you will be able to tell more easily when your starter is "hungry." When the starter looks like it is falling instead of rising, or if it is becoming more runny when fed, you should feed it more frequently.

Repeat the process of feeding once daily. As the days go on, your starter should start to develop more bubbling and a sourdough smell. It should also start to become hungrier, requiring feedings twice a day (once in the morning and once at night).

As you continue to feed the starter, a second container will come in handy. By moving the starter from one container to the other during feedings, you can see the rising and falling more easily. If you continue to use only one container, it will become clouded with flour and it will be trickier to observe the rising process.

One to two weeks later, once your starter is alive and well, use the float test to see if you are ready to bake: Drop a spoonful of starter into a bowl of water. If the starter floats, it is ready to use in any recipe that calls for sourdough starter.

When you aren't going to be baking as much and want to start feeding your starter less, you can keep it alive in the refrigerator, feeding it just once a week. At this point, you should feed it on the same day each week to keep it consistent and stable.

Sourdough Starter Discard Crepes

Once you start on starter, don't stop! Crepes are one of the best things you can make from starter discard because of their flexibility. And when it comes to the crepes, feel free to get creative with toppings and fillings—we love using whipped cream and blueberries, but you can of course use any fresh fruit you please, or a simple treatment of lemon juice and sugar or cinnamon sugar. As the crepes come off the skillet, set them on parchment paper to prevent sticking, and cover them with a kitchen towel to help keep them warm and soft. Depending on what phase your starter is in, you can save the discard in the refrigerator over the course of a few feedings until you have a full cup.

MAKES 8 CREPES

1 cup starter discard
(see page 245)

¼ cup whole milk

1 large egg

1 teaspoon pure vanilla
extract

½ teaspoon kosher salt

½ cup heavy cream

1 to 2 tablespoons unsalted
butter

1 pint blueberries

Confectioners' sugar
(optional)

In a large bowl, whisk together the starter discard, milk, egg, vanilla, and salt until smooth. Cover with plastic wrap and refrigerate for 1 hour.

Meanwhile, whip the cream (by hand or using an electric mixer) in a medium bowl until doubled in volume and soft peaks form, 3 to 5 minutes. Cover with plastic wrap and refrigerate until ready to serve.

In a nonstick medium skillet, melt the butter over medium-low heat. Use a ¼-cup measure to scoop the batter into the skillet and tilt the pan to coat the bottom. Once the edges of the crepe are crispy and the top is set, about 2 minutes, flip the crepe and cook until the bottom is lightly golden, 30 seconds more. Set the finished crepe on parchment paper and cover with a towel. Repeat with the remaining batter.

To serve, slide the crepes onto plates and place a dollop of whipped cream in the center of each crepe. Top with the blueberries and roll each into a long cylinder. Dust lightly with confectioners' sugar, if desired, and serve with any additional whipped cream alongside.

Super Garlic Kimchi

Homemade kimchi can change your life—it's healthy, full of flavor, easy on the budget, lasts forever in the refrigerator (okay, 3 to 6 months), and only gets tastier with time. The beauty of this recipe is that it is meant to be flexible—experiment with different vegetables and tweak it to your liking as you go. A few notes on ingredients: Sweet rice flour, also known as glutinous rice flour, is an important component in kimchi to make the marinade easy to spread (it's gluten-free but named for its consistency). Korean radish, or mu, *is a short, fat, dense white radish, which adds a nice textural crunch and peppery flavor. Daikon is a fine substitute. And finally,* gochugaru *is Korean red pepper flakes, sold in mild or spicy varieties. Be careful to buy the flakes and not the powder (*gochujangyong gochugaru*), which is sold in similar packaging. Unused* gochugaru *can be stored in a zip-top bag in the freezer for up to 6 months.*

MAKES ABOUT 6 POUNDS

2 medium heads napa cabbage (about 4½ pounds), halved lengthwise

1½ cups coarse sea salt

1½ cups fine sea salt

2 tablespoons sweet rice flour

2 pounds Korean radishes or daikon radishes, cut into matchsticks

2½ cups gochugaru (Korean red pepper flakes)

1 cup minced garlic

1½ tablespoons minced fresh ginger

1½ cups fish sauce

2 tablespoons sugar

1 pound scallions, cut into 1-inch pieces

Generously season the cut sides of the cabbages with the coarse sea salt, opening the leaves to make sure the salt gets in between them. In a large bowl or roasting pan, combine 1 gallon water with the fine sea salt and whisk to dissolve. Place the cabbages cut-side up in the salt brine and set aside at room temperature for 6 to 8 hours. After 3 hours, turn the cabbages over so they are cut-side down.

Remove the cabbages from the brine, rinse, and transfer to a colander cut-side down. Let drain for at least 1 hour.

In a medium saucepan, combine 1 cup water and the sweet rice flour and stir to combine well. Set over medium heat and cook, stir-

CONTINUED

ring constantly, until the mixture resembles a sticky paste, almost like glue. Bring the mixture to a boil, then remove from the heat and let cool.

In a large bowl, toss together the radishes and the gochugaru. Let sit for 5 minutes until the radishes turn red. Add the garlic, ginger, fish sauce, and sugar and toss to combine. Add the scallions and the rice flour mixture and stir to combine. Set aside for 1 hour.

Rub the mixture into each cabbage leaf, starting from the core of the cabbage and working to the tip, coating both sides while keeping the core intact. Fold the coated cabbage in half to create a tight bundle and transfer the 4 cabbage halves to an airtight container.

Cover the container and set aside to ferment at room temperature for 2 to 3 days. You should start to see some bubbles on the second day. (Fermenting progresses more quickly in warmer temperatures, so it might take longer or shorter depending on the climate where you are.)

When small bubbles are visible in the brine and the cabbage is tangy, divide it among airtight containers and store refrigerated for 3 to 6 months.

Cleanliness in Fermenting

Fermentation is the natural process of microorganisms like yeast and bacteria breaking down substances to create things like kimchi, cheese, beer, wine, bread, and lots of other delicious foods. It's super important to start with clean equipment so you don't end up with bad *bacteria and dirt—not from the food—in there. Before you begin, use soap and hot water to thoroughly clean any surfaces you'll be working on and any equipment or storage containers you'll be using. Don't forget your hands, too! If you really get into this process, you can find fermentation crocks, weights, and other devices such as airlocks.*

Pink Sauerkraut

You might hear sauerkraut *and think of canned goods that have been at the back of your pantry for a few years, but we'd like to change that narrative. The salt ratio is super important for fermentation here, so we recommend using a scale. For this recipe, we like a good level of saltiness, so we go with a 3 percent salt by weight ratio. Weigh the shredded cabbage, then multiply that weight by 0.03 to calculate the weight of salt needed. (Alternatively, you can weigh the cabbage at the grocery store and use 4 to 5 teaspoons per pound.)*

MAKES ABOUT 2 QUARTS

1 to 2 heads red cabbage, cut into uniform strips

Kosher salt (see headnote)

Fresh lemon juice (1 tablespoon per pound)

In a large bowl, toss the cabbage with the salt, rubbing it into the nooks and crannies of the leaves. Using your hands, massage the leaves until the cabbage has released enough liquid to submerge the leaves completely, 7 to 10 minutes.

Add the lemon juice and toss to coat. The mixture should immediately turn pink; over the course of fermentation, the sauerkraut will turn an even brighter rosy hue.

Transfer the cabbage and liquid to a large glass jar, pushing the cabbage down to make sure it is completely covered, leaving an inch or two of room at the top of the jar. Push an open plastic bag (with no holes in it) into the empty space inside the jar and fold the edges of the bag over the rim of the jar. Secure the bag with a rubber band and fill the bag up to the top of the jar with water. This method creates an airproof seal but allows carbon dioxide to be released during the fermentation.

Place the jar in a dark, warm (70°F to 80°F) place. Some slight bubbling will begin within 2 to 3 days, and it will continue to ferment for around 14 days. Check in once a day, making sure that the cabbage is always fully submerged to prevent mold from forming. Give the jar a shake once a day and push all the cabbage under the brine as necessary. (If mold forms or the sauerkraut becomes slimy and putrid, discard and start over.) The sauerkraut is ready to eat when the cabbage is soft and tangy. After opening, the sauerkraut will keep for up to 2 months in the refrigerator.

Rainbow Escabeche

Escabeche is the Spanish word for "pickle." While it's often applied to marinating meat or fish in acidic vinegar or citrus juice, we like to give the escabeche treatment to vegetables. This combination of orange and purple cauliflower as well as carrots and green beans makes a pucker-worthy rainbow. You'll need three clean 1-quart jars with lids, and you'll want to cut the vegetables into roughly same-size pieces to ensure even preservation. The finished product will be a welcome accompaniment to nearly any meal that you otherwise would have served with plain ol' pickles.

MAKES 3 QUARTS

½ medium red onion, roughly chopped

6 jalapeños, roughly chopped (seeded if desired)

1 shallot, roughly chopped

2 cups roughly chopped purple cauliflower florets

2 cups roughly chopped orange cauliflower florets

2 cups sliced carrots (about 4 carrots)

8 ounces green beans, trimmed and roughly chopped

6 garlic cloves, peeled

1 tablespoon black peppercorns

¼ cup kosher salt

1 tablespoon sugar

3 bay leaves

2 tablespoons dried Mexican oregano

4 cups 5% acidity vinegar, such as distilled white, red wine vinegar, or apple cider vinegar

In a large bowl, toss together the onion, jalapeños, shallot, both cauliflowers, the carrots, and green beans to combine well. Fill three 1-quart glass jars with the vegetable mixture, leaving about 1 inch of space at the top of each jar.

In a large saucepan, bring 4 cups water to a boil. Add the garlic, peppercorns, salt, sugar, bay leaves, and oregano. Cook, stirring until the salt and sugar are completely dissolved and the peppercorns and bay leaves are very fragrant.

Add the vinegar (don't worry if the mixture suddenly smells sour) and bring the mixture back to a boil. Carefully transfer the mixture to a spouted measuring cup, then pour the brine into the jars, filling each jar to the top, making sure to evenly distribute the garlic, bay leaves, and peppercorns among them.

Seal the jars and let cool to room temperature before transferring them to the refrigerator. Let the escabeche cure for 2 days in the refrigerator, at which point the vegetables will be soft and pickled. Store the escabeche refrigerated in the jars for up to 2 months unopened, or 1 month after opening.

Sweet and Sour Pickled Radishes

Radishes are always utterly gorgeous additions to salads and sandwiches, but these intensely delicious pickled radishes take everything up a notch—never underestimate the power of vinegar, sugar, and salt. If you can't find the mix of radishes we call for here, just use any combination you can find. Slicing them up is the perfect job for a mandoline if you have one, as you can choose the thickness and it will ensure even slices, but you can also use a very sharp knife and work carefully!

MAKES ABOUT 3 CUPS

¼ cup distilled white vinegar

¼ cup sugar

1 teaspoon kosher salt

3 cups very thinly sliced watermelon, red, and/or green radishes

In a small bowl, combine the vinegar, sugar, and salt and whisk until the sugar and salt have dissolved.

Pack the radishes into a large (1 quart) glass jar. Pour the vinegar mixture over the radishes, making sure they are submerged, and seal the jar. Transfer to the refrigerator and let the radishes cure for at least 2 hours or overnight.

When the radishes are nicely sour and the brine is vibrant in color, the radishes are ready to eat. Store refrigerated for up to 1 month.

Refrigerator Pickles

Sometimes you just want a plain old dill pickle. This is our foolproof, go-to, low-maintenance recipe for classic pickled cucumbers, though it'll work well with other vegetables if you feel like experimenting. If you want to get creative, you can play with the aromatics, too—try mixing it up with fresh herbs like thyme or cilantro, or different vinegars like apple cider or red wine.

MAKES 3 QUARTS

2 pounds ice

18 Kirby cucumbers

3 tablespoons extra-virgin olive oil

½ medium yellow onion, diced

½ large carrot, diced

1 celery stalk, diced

3 garlic cloves, minced

1 tablespoon sugar

2 teaspoons fennel seeds

¼ teaspoon crushed red pepper flakes

5 black peppercorns

1 teaspoon coriander seeds

1 teaspoon yellow mustard seeds

2 teaspoons kosher salt

2 quarts distilled white vinegar

12 to 18 sprigs fresh dill

Place the ice in a large bowl. Add the cucumbers, then fill with enough water to cover. Let soak for about 10 minutes to cool.

In a large saucepan, heat the olive oil over medium heat. Add the onion, carrot, celery, and garlic and cook, stirring occasionally, until the vegetables are lightly golden, 3 to 5 minutes. Add the sugar, fennel seeds, pepper flakes, black peppercorns, coriander seeds, mustard seeds, and salt and cook, stirring, until the spices are toasted and fragrant, about 2 minutes. Add 2 cups water and the vinegar and bring to a boil, then reduce to a simmer.

Meanwhile, drain the cucumbers and divide evenly among three 1-quart glass jars. Add the dill to the jars, dividing evenly.

Remove the brine from the heat and carefully pour the mixture into the jars, making sure the cucumbers are completely covered. Seal the jars and let cool to room temperature before transferring them to the refrigerator. Let the cucumbers cure for at least 4 hours and up to 24 hours, until they are soft and nicely sour.

Strawberry-Chile Jam

We can think of no better way to preserve summer's beautiful berry bounty than turning plump strawberries into jam. And we can think of no better way to kick that jam up a notch than adding in red pepper flakes. The jam is sweet, hot, and perfect on flaky biscuits, with creamy cheese and crackers, slathered on a sandwich . . . and we won't tell anyone if you just eat it straight off the spoon.

MAKES 1½ TO 2 CUPS

1 pound strawberries, hulled and roughly chopped

1 cup sugar

¼ cup fresh lemon juice

1 to 2 tablespoons crushed red pepper flakes

Pinch of kosher salt

In a heavy-bottomed saucepan, combine the strawberries, sugar, lemon juice, pepper flakes, and salt. Cook over medium-low heat, stirring constantly, until the sugar dissolves, about 2 minutes. Bring the mixture to a simmer, stirring frequently, and cook until it is thick enough to coat the back of a spoon, 10 to 15 minutes. Remove from the heat and let cool.

Store refrigerated in an airtight container for up to 2 weeks.

Limoncello

Listen up, limoncello lovers: you don't have to be in Italy, or even at an Italian restaurant, to enjoy this after-dinner liqueur. Limoncello is as easy to make at home as it is delicious, and believe it or not, it takes just about 30 minutes of prep time. You'll need a 2-liter glass canning jar, and we recommend a dark, cool, rarely used cupboard for this stuff to hang out. If you use a higher proof alcohol, such as 190-proof, you won't need to allow as much time for infusing (and will be able to freeze your finished product—see Note). Some say you can drink the limoncello the day after mixing in the simple syrup, some say it needs to mellow for another 30 days. This is our version. Salute!

MAKES 2 LITERS

10 to 12 unwaxed organic lemons, scrubbed (see Note, page 266)

1 (750 ml) bottle 100-proof or higher clear grain alcohol, such as Everclear

4⅓ cups filtered water, plus more as needed

3¼ cups sugar

Using a vegetable peeler, peel the lemon zest into long strips, making sure to avoid the bitter white pith. If you accidentally get some pith attached to your peel, use a sharp knife to gently scrape it off.

Place the peels in a 2-liter glass canning jar and pour in the alcohol to cover. Give the jar a swirl to combine and set aside in a cool, dark place, such as a rarely used cabinet, to infuse. Swirl the jar once daily. The alcohol will turn yellow and the zests will lighten. The mixture is ready when the alcohol is deep yellow and the zests are almost white, at least 14 days, or preferably between 20 and 30 for the best flavor.

Once the alcohol is infused, make the simple syrup: In a large deep pot, bring the filtered water barely to a boil over medium heat. Stir in the sugar. Cook, whisking constantly, until the sugar is dissolved, taking care not to boil the mixture once the sugar is added or the simple syrup will be cloudy. Remove the pot from the heat and let cool.

CONTINUED

Meanwhile, strain the infused alcohol through a fine-mesh sieve into a large bowl.

Discard the lemon zests and rinse out the jar. Set the sieve on top of the jar and line it with cheesecloth or an unbleached, flat-bottomed coffee filter. (If the opening of the glass jar is too small, place a funnel on top of the glass jar to hold the sieve in place.) Slowly pour the lemon alcohol back into the glass container (or use a ladle). Repeat this straining process once or twice more, slowly pouring back and forth until there is little to no debris caught in your cheesecloth.

When the simple syrup is cool, measure out 750 milliliters into a liquid measuring cup and set the rest aside. In a large bowl, combine the 750 milliliters of simple syrup with the alcohol. Taste it for sweetness and add water or more simple syrup as needed. Pour the limoncello back into the glass jar and note the date on the jar. Store in a cool, dark place for 14 more days.

When it has aged for 14 days, or longer to your taste, use a funnel to pour the limoncello into a glass bottle or other storage bottle and chill in the fridge before serving. It will keep refrigerated for up to 1 month or frozen for up to 6 months (see Note).

NOTE: If you used 190-proof (95% ABV) alcohol, you can store the limoncello in the freezer. If you used anything lower proof, it needs to be stored in the fridge, as it would freeze otherwise. The flavor of the limoncello will be better at refrigerator temperature, so if you do store it in the freezer, put it in the fridge an hour or so before serving for the best taste.

Preserved Lemons

Lemons pack power in the kitchen—always keep them on hand if you can—and Meyer lemons are extra special, though their season is short-lived. This recipe preserves their classic flavor by curing them in salt with plenty of thyme so that you can pull them out of your fridge anytime you need to add a punch to stews, soups, and salad dressings. We recommend a 1-quart glass jar with a rubber seal, as the salt and acid from the lemons will usually start breaking down and corroding a metal lid.

MAKES 1 QUART

1½ pounds unwaxed Meyer lemons (about 8), scrubbed (see Note)

¼ cup kosher salt

3 garlic cloves

6 to 9 sprigs fresh thyme

4 bay leaves

1 tablespoon black peppercorns

½ to 1 cup fresh lemon juice, plus more as needed

Halve the lemons lengthwise but only go three-quarters of the way down, stopping just before cutting all the way through. Give the lemons a quarter-turn and make another cut down each lemon at right angles to the first cut crosswise, again stopping before cutting all the way through. (You are cutting the shape of a cross in each lemon but leaving the rind intact at one end to keep the lemon together.)

Spread the lemons open like flowers and sprinkle salt into the centers, covering all the lemon flesh.

Pack the lemons into a 1-quart glass jar (it's okay to smush them to fit), adding the garlic, thyme, bay leaves, and peppercorns in layers between them. Pour the lemon juice into the jar to cover everything. (Add more lemon juice if needed to cover.) Seal the jar.

Place the jar in a warm, dark place to begin the fermentation process.

Open the jar daily to release gases and pressure, then reseal the jar and flip a few times. Continue this process until the lemons are very soft and the brine is syrupy, 10 to 14 days. (If the jar has developed mold on the top, or the lemons start to get a bad smell, discard and start again.) Store the lemons refrigerated for up to 6 months.

NOTE: Since the citrus peels are key here, it is best to use unwaxed organic fruit if possible. Check your local farmers' market, or even better, pluck them from a tree if that's available to you. If they are waxed, soak the fruit whole in a bowl of warm water with a bit of vinegar and baking soda mixed in. Soak the fruit for about 20 minutes, then scrub clean.

Acknowledgments

It takes a village—and sometimes a whole city—to write a book. Thanks to . . .

The members of the Tastemade team whose support and hard work made this book a reality:

Lauren Arso

Sarah Anne Bargatze

Sarah Beaumont

Amanda Dameron

Paul Delmont

Natalie Jones

Emma Niles

Megahn Perry

Jeremy Strauss

Tyler Wildermuth

The recipe writers, developers, and testers in our wonderful community, without whom there'd be nothing to eat:

Danielle Campbell

Casey Elsass

Tarveen Forrester

Jay Holzer

Nicole Iizuka

Tal Itzkovitch

Rob Kloth

Keven Matsuzaka

Masanori Matsuzaka

Alba Molina

Alyssa Noui

Gabe Rubin

Molly Schmidt

Heejin Suh

Karla T. Vasquez

Jessica Wang

Jaclyn Wilson

Murad Yasin

Amanda Englander, for helping us get this book across the finish line.

Eve Attermann, our agent at WME.

The team at Clarkson Potter:

Chloe Aryeh

Jessica Heim

Mia Johnson

Lydia O'Brien

Joyce Wong

Natalia Yera

Index

Note: Page references in *italics* indicate photographs.

Cover design: Bryce de Flamand
Cover photograph: Ashley Corbin-Teich
Back cover photographs: Ashley Corbin-Teich and Paul Delmont